The Master Builder Book of Wix Website Development and Design for Seniors and Beginners:

Step-by-Step Instructions to Help You Build a Stunning Website Easily

Stanley Duxton

Table of Contents

Introduction

Creating a website might seem like a daunting task, especially if you're a senior or someone who is just starting their journey into the world of web development. However, with the right tools, guidance, and a bit of patience, anyone can create a beautiful, functional website, regardless of their experience level. This book is designed to help you navigate the process of website creation using one of the most user-friendly platforms available today—Wix.

Building your website can open up a world of possibilities. Whether you're looking to showcase your hobbies, share important information, or even create a business presence online, having a website is a powerful way to achieve your goals. Wix makes this process incredibly accessible, offering a range of customizable templates and easy-to-use tools that allow you to design a website exactly how you envision it. This book serves as your companion, guiding you through every step of the way as you build and manage your very own website using Wix.

The Purpose of the Book

This book is not just another technical manual; it's a comprehensive guide meant to empower you to take control of your digital presence. Designed with seniors and beginners in mind, it aims to demystify the complexities of website creation and make the process as simple and enjoyable as possible. You don't need to have any prior experience with web design or development to benefit from this guide. Whether you're entirely new to building websites or have some basic knowledge, this book will walk you through everything you need to know in a clear, straightforward manner.

The goal is to ensure that by the end of this book, you feel confident in your ability to create, design, and manage your website on Wix. We'll explore the essentials of web design and development, from setting up your account and choosing the right template to fine-tuning your site and publishing it online. Additionally, we'll cover maintenance tips and tricks to ensure that your website stays fresh and functional in the long run.

Wix is a platform that prides itself on simplicity, and we will leverage that simplicity in this guide. By breaking down the process into digestible steps, this book will enable you to achieve your goals without feeling overwhelmed. With Wix's drag-and-drop functionality and a wealth of pre-designed templates at your disposal, building a website is no longer reserved for web designers or tech experts. It's now accessible to anyone willing to give it a try, and this book is here to make sure you succeed.

What You Will Learn

As you progress through this book, you'll be introduced to the core elements of website creation. You'll learn how to select and customize templates, choose the right color schemes and fonts, and organize your site to ensure it provides a user-friendly experience. We'll also explore how to add essential elements to your site, such as text, images, and videos, and discuss how to integrate useful features like contact forms, social media buttons, and online store options.

One of the most important skills you'll acquire is how to maintain your website effectively. A website isn't a one-time project—it needs regular updates, tweaks, and monitoring to keep it running smoothly. Whether it's adjusting the content, checking for broken links, or adding fresh media, maintenance is key to keeping your site relevant and effective. We'll cover the best practices for website maintenance, ensuring that your site remains polished and functional for as long as you need it.

Additionally, this book will provide insights into more advanced features, such as improving your site's visibility through search engine optimization (SEO), creating a blog or portfolio, and even setting up an online store if you wish to sell products. The tips provided throughout this book are designed to help you not only build a website but also grow and enhance it over time.

The beauty of this guide is that you won't be expected to become a web development expert overnight. The focus is on making the process simple and enjoyable, allowing you to create a professional-looking website without getting bogged down by technical jargon or complex coding. We'll focus on the tools and techniques that matter most to you, helping you navigate the learning curve in a manageable way.

Who This Book is For

This book is primarily aimed at seniors and beginners who are new to website creation and might feel apprehensive about diving into something that may seem too complicated. If you've never built a website before or have limited experience, this guide is exactly what you need to get started.

Whether you're looking to create a personal blog, an online portfolio, or even a business website, this book will give you the knowledge and skills you need. The step-by-step instructions are designed to be clear and easy to follow, ensuring that you can make progress without feeling overwhelmed.

If you've been wanting to create a website but have been putting it off because you think it's too difficult or time-consuming, this book will help you realize that website creation doesn't need to be intimidating. Wix's user-friendly platform makes it possible for anyone, regardless of age or technical experience, to create a site they can be proud of.

Additionally, suppose you are a senior looking to explore the digital world and stay connected with family, friends, or even customers. In that case, this book will be your guide to confidently stepping into the online space. With technology becoming an integral part of everyday life, having a website is a great way to stay connected, share information, and express yourself in the digital realm.

How This Book is Structured

The structure of this book has been designed to ensure that the learning process is as smooth and intuitive as possible. Each chapter builds upon the previous one, gradually introducing new concepts and features to avoid overwhelming you with too much information at once. Whether you choose to read the book from start to finish or jump to specific chapters that interest you most, the content will be easy to follow and immediately applicable.

We begin by covering the very basics, ensuring that you understand the fundamentals of Wix, the design process, and the overall goals of building a website. From there, we dive deeper into the hands-on aspects of creating your site, such as customizing templates, adding content, and incorporating special features like social media links and contact forms.

As you progress through the chapters, you'll also discover how to fine-tune your website's design and functionality, giving you the tools you need to maintain it effectively once it's up and running. We'll even touch on more advanced topics, such as SEO and the integration of third-party apps, allowing you to expand your website's capabilities if you choose.

The book is designed to be interactive, with practical tips and examples provided throughout each section. As you go through the chapters, you'll have the opportunity to apply what you've learned in real time, building your website step by step. This approach ensures that you not only understand the concepts being taught but also gain the hands-on experience needed to master them.

By the end of this book, you'll be well-equipped to build and maintain a website using Wix, regardless of your experience level. Whether you're a senior looking to explore the digital world or a beginner who wants to create a professional website with minimal effort, this guide will provide you with all the tools, knowledge, and confidence you need to succeed. Get ready to unlock your potential and create a stunning website that's uniquely yours!

Certainly! Below is a detailed content for *Chapter 1: Understanding Wix and Web Design Basics.* It's structured around the subheadings you've provided and written to ensure a smooth narrative flow. The content is paraphrased and tailored for a beginner-friendly audience, making it ideal for seniors and those new to web design.

Chapter 1: Understanding Wix and Web Design Basics

In today's digital age, having a website is more important than ever. Whether you're looking to start a personal blog, showcase your hobbies, or build an online business, a website can be your window to the world. However, for many, the idea of creating a website can be overwhelming, especially when faced with complex coding languages and design principles. This is where Wix comes in—a platform designed to make website creation simple and accessible for everyone, regardless of their experience level.

Introduction to Wix: What is Wix, and why is it a great platform for beginners and seniors?

Wix is an online website-building platform that allows anyone, regardless of their technical skill level, to create a website. Unlike traditional website development that requires knowledge of coding languages like HTML, CSS, or JavaScript, Wix simplifies the process with its user-friendly, drag-and-drop interface. This makes it an ideal choice for seniors and beginners who want to create a website without diving into the complexities of programming.

One of the main reasons Wix stands out is its accessibility. The platform is entirely cloud-based, meaning you don't need to worry about installing any software or managing web hosting services. Everything you need is in one place, and all you need is an internet connection and a device to get started.

Wix offers a range of features that make the process easy and intuitive, even for people who have never built a website before. You can choose from hundreds of customizable templates, each designed to fit a wide variety of purposes—from business websites to portfolios, blogs, and online stores. These templates are fully customizable, allowing you to create a website that matches your unique style and needs.

Another standout feature of Wix is its drag-and-drop editor. This feature eliminates the need to write any code, which can often be intimidating for those new to web design. With Wix's editor, you can click on the elements you want to add to your website, such as text boxes, images, buttons, and more, and place them exactly where you want them on the page. The interface is simple, intuitive, and designed to make the process as easy as possible.

For seniors or beginners who might be worried about technology, Wix also offers excellent customer support. Whether you have a question about customizing your website or you encounter a technical issue, Wix provides numerous resources to help you find the answers you need. There's a robust help center, live chat support, and a comprehensive knowledge base available to guide you through every step of your website-building journey.

The Role of a Website: Understanding the importance of having an online presence

In today's world, a website is more than just a digital business card or portfolio. It's your gateway to the online world and serves as the first point of contact for potential visitors or customers. Whether you're a senior looking to stay connected with family and friends, an artist hoping to showcase your work, or a small business owner looking to expand your reach, a website plays a crucial role in establishing your online presence.

Having a website can help you:

1. **Reach a Wider Audience**: The internet is a global network, and a website allows you to connect with people from all over the world. Whether you're blogging about your favorite hobbies or starting a business, having a website gives you the platform to reach a much larger audience than social media or local advertising alone.

2. **Build Credibility**: A well-designed website can enhance your credibility and make you look more professional. Whether you're a small business owner, a consultant, or an artist, having a website establishes you as a serious player in your field and gives people a place to learn more about you and your services.

3. **Showcase Your Work or Interests**: If you're a senior with a passion for photography, cooking, or writing, a website can be the perfect place to showcase your work and share it with the world. A website allows you to curate your content, display your achievements, and create an online portfolio.

4. **Connect with Others**: A website allows you to engage with your audience through comments, blogs, and contact forms. It's a place for people to reach out, ask questions, and connect with you.

5. **Control Your Online Identity**: In the digital age, many aspects of your life are accessible online. Having a website allows you to control the information about you that appears on the internet. You can ensure that your online presence aligns with your values and interests.

6. **Expand Your Business**: A website is essential for those looking to start or grow a business. It acts as a virtual storefront, allowing you to sell products, attract customers, and promote your services. A website also helps you manage your brand and customer relations more effectively.

Understanding the importance of having a website is the first step in realizing its benefits for your personal or professional life. Once you recognize its role, you'll be motivated to create a site that reflects your unique goals and aspirations.

Wix Features Overview: Key features like templates, drag-and-drop editor, and mobile responsiveness

Wix is packed with features that make website creation quick, easy, and effective. Here's an overview of some of the key features that set Wix apart from other website-building platforms:

1. **Templates**: Wix offers hundreds of professionally designed templates that cater to a wide range of industries, interests, and needs. Whether you're creating a blog, an online store, a personal portfolio, or a business website, you'll find a template that suits your vision. These templates are fully customizable, so you can adjust colors, fonts, and layouts to make the design your own.

2. **Drag-and-Drop Editor**: One of Wix's most popular features is its drag-and-drop editor, which makes it incredibly easy to add elements to your website. You can click on a text box, image, button, or other element and drag it to where you want it on the page. The editor allows

you to visually design your website without needing any coding skills. This feature is perfect for seniors or beginners who may find traditional web development techniques intimidating.

3. **Mobile Responsiveness**: As more people browse the web on their smartphones, websites need to be mobile-friendly. Wix ensures that your website will look great on any device by automatically adjusting the design for mobile screens. This means your website will be just as functional and visually appealing on a smartphone as it is on a desktop computer.

4. **App Market**: Wix has an extensive app market where you can add extra functionality to your website. From live chat options to booking systems, you can easily install apps that will enhance the user experience and streamline your website's operations. These apps are designed to be easy to install and use, even for those with no prior technical experience.

5. **SEO Tools**: Wix offers built-in SEO tools that help your website rank higher in search engine

results. SEO, or search engine optimization, is the practice of improving your website's visibility on search engines like Google. With Wix, you can easily optimize your website's content by adding keywords, meta tags, and descriptions to improve search rankings and attract more visitors.

6. **E-commerce Features**: If you're looking to sell products or services online, Wix provides powerful e-commerce tools that let you create a fully functioning online store. You can add products, set up secure payment gateways, and track inventory—all without needing to know any code. Wix's e-commerce platform is designed to be intuitive, so you can start selling quickly.

7. **Analytics**: Wix provides built-in analytics that allow you to track the performance of your website. You can see how many people are visiting your site, which pages they're viewing, and how they're interacting with your content. This data is invaluable for understanding your audience and improving your site's performance over time.

Key Terms in Web Design: Explaining essential web design terminology such as domains, hosting, layouts, and navigation

Before you dive into creating your Wix website, it's important to understand some essential web design terms that will help you navigate the platform more effectively. Here are a few key terms to know:

1. **Domain**: A domain is the web address (URL) that people use to find your website. For example, "www.yourwebsite.com" is your domain name. Wix allows you to either use a free domain that's provided by Wix (which will include "wixsite" in the URL) or you can purchase a custom domain to make your website look more professional. Having a custom domain is a great way to build credibility and make your website easier to remember.

2. **Hosting**: Hosting refers to the service that stores your website's files and makes them accessible on the internet. Wix handles all of the hosting for you, so you don't need to worry

about finding a hosting provider or managing servers. This makes it even easier to get started with your website without technical hassle.

3. **Layout**: Your website's layout refers to the arrangement of elements on each page, including where the text, images, and buttons are placed. Wix offers a variety of layout options through its templates, but you can customize the layout to suit your needs. A clean, well-organized layout helps ensure that visitors can easily navigate your site and find the information they're looking for.

4. **Navigation**: Navigation refers to the system that allows visitors to move between different pages on your website. A well-organized navigation menu is crucial for user experience. It should be easy to find and understand, so visitors can quickly access the content they're interested in. Wix lets you create simple, intuitive navigation menus that make it easy for visitors to explore your site.

With these key features and terms in mind, you're well on your way to understanding the basics of web design and how Wix can help you bring your ideas to life. As we move forward in this book, you'll gain hands-on experience using these tools to create and customize your website, ensuring it meets your needs and reflects your unique vision.

Certainly! Below is a detailed version of *Chapter 2: Getting Started with Wix*. This content is designed for beginners and seniors to help them understand how to create and manage their Wix accounts, navigate the dashboard, select a template, and use the drag-and-drop editor to customize their site. The content has been written in a continuous narrative to ensure it flows smoothly without interruptions.

Chapter 2: Getting Started with Wix

Building a website may feel like a huge task, but with Wix, it's incredibly easy to get started. This chapter will walk you through the initial steps of signing up for Wix, setting up your account, navigating the platform's features, and choosing the perfect template for your website. You'll also get a detailed introduction to the Wix Editor, where you'll be able to create and customize your website using simple drag-and-drop tools.

By the end of this chapter, you'll have a clear understanding of the Wix platform and how to navigate its features to start building your website with confidence.

Creating Your Wix Account: How to sign up and set up your Wix account

The first step in getting started with Wix is creating an account. Setting up an account on Wix is quick, straightforward, and free. Let's go through the steps to get you signed up and ready to begin your website creation journey.

1. **Go to Wix.com**: Open your internet browser and go to www.wix.com. Once the page loads, you'll see a "Get Started" button or a prompt to sign up. Click on it to begin the registration process.

2. **Sign Up for an Account**: You will be asked to sign up for an account. You can create a new account by entering your email address and a password, or you can sign up using your Facebook or Google account. Signing up via Google or Facebook is a convenient option if you already have an account with either of these services.

3. **Choose Your Account Type**: Wix will ask you whether you're building a personal website or a business website. Depending on your goals, select the appropriate option. If you're not sure which one to choose, you can always change it later. Wix offers a variety of templates for both personal and business websites, so this selection is to help guide you through the options.

4. **Verify Your Email**: After signing up, Wix will send a verification email to the address you

provided. Open the email and click on the verification link to confirm your account. This step ensures that your email address is valid and helps secure your Wix account.

5. **Set Up Your Profile**: Once your account is verified, Wix will prompt you to set up your profile. You may need to enter some basic details, such as your name and business name (if applicable). This information helps Wix tailor your experience and recommend suitable templates for your needs.

Now that you've created your account, you're ready to start building your website. Wix will guide you through the setup process with a few prompts, but let's dive deeper into the Wix dashboard next.

Exploring the Dashboard: A walkthrough of the Wix dashboard and how to navigate it

Once your Wix account is set up, you'll be directed to the Wix dashboard, which serves as the central hub for managing all aspects of your website. The dashboard can seem a little overwhelming at first glance, but with a little exploration, you'll find it's designed to be easy to use and intuitive.

Let's break down the main elements of the dashboard so you can start navigating it with ease.

1. **The Site Manager**: The first thing you'll notice on the dashboard is the "Site Manager" section. This area displays all the websites you've created or worked on in your Wix account. If you've just signed up, you'll likely see a prompt to start a new website. From here, you can also choose to manage existing websites, view their stats, or access editing tools.

2. **The Editor Button**: This is where the magic happens! When you're ready to start building or editing your site, click the "Editor" button on the dashboard. This takes you to the Wix Editor, where you can customize every aspect of your website, from the layout to the color scheme to the content itself.

3. **The Templates Tab**: If you want to change your template or explore other options, you can click on the "Templates" tab. Wix offers hundreds of professionally designed templates,

and this section allows you to browse them by category. You'll also be able to search for templates based on keywords, which makes it easy to find something specific to your needs, whether it's a blog, portfolio, or business website.

4. **The Apps & Marketing Section**: Wix also has an extensive app market that allows you to add functionality to your site, such as booking systems, contact forms, or live chat features. You can find this in the "Apps & Marketing" section of the dashboard. Here, you can browse apps that integrate directly with Wix to help you enhance your site's functionality. Marketing tools, such as email campaigns and SEO tools, are also accessible from this section.

5. **Account Settings**: In the upper right corner of your dashboard, you'll see a profile icon. Clicking on this will open a dropdown menu with options to adjust your account settings, change your password, access billing information, and more.

Now that you know your way around the Wix dashboard, the next important step is choosing the right template for your website.

Choosing Your Template: How to choose the right template based on your goals and business needs

Choosing the right template is a crucial first step in building your website. Wix offers hundreds of professionally designed templates, each created for a specific type of website. Whether you're building a personal blog, an online store, or a portfolio, you'll find a template designed to suit your goals.

Here are a few steps and tips to help you choose the perfect template:

1. **Identify Your Goals**: Before you start browsing templates, consider the purpose of your website. What do you want it to achieve? Are you looking to create an online store, display a personal portfolio, or share your thoughts through a blog? Knowing your website's purpose will help you narrow down the template options to those that best align with your goals.

2. **Browse by Category**: Wix allows you to browse templates by category, such as business, blog, portfolio, online store, and more. Browse through the categories and take note of templates that appeal to you. You can preview the template before selecting it to ensure it aligns with your needs.

3. **Consider Your Branding**: When selecting a template, think about your brand or style. If you're creating a business website, you'll want a clean, professional-looking template that reflects your brand identity. For a personal website or portfolio, you might choose something visually creative or artistic. Wix templates are highly customizable, so even if a template doesn't perfectly match your vision, you can tweak it to suit your preferences.

4. **Choose a Template with the Right Features**: Some templates come with built-in features, such as contact forms, galleries, or product pages. Make sure to select a template that has the features you need for your website. For example, if you're building an online store, you'll want a template with e-commerce

functionality that allows you to add products, set up payment methods, and manage orders.

5. **Preview the Template**: Once you've narrowed down your choices, click on a template to preview it. This allows you to see how it looks and functions. You can explore how the layout works, how easy it is to navigate, and how the content is arranged. Don't rush this step—take the time to make sure the template feels right for your website.

6. **Start Customizing**: Once you've selected a template, you can start customizing it to match your vision. Wix's drag-and-drop editor makes it easy to adjust everything from the color scheme and fonts to the placement of images and text.

Understanding Wix Editor: Introduction to the drag-and-drop editor and how to use it effectively

The Wix Editor is where you'll spend most of your time while creating and customizing your website. It's designed to be easy to use, even for those with little to no experience in web design. The drag-and-drop interface allows you to place elements exactly where you want them, without having to write any code. Let's take a look at how to use the Wix Editor effectively.

1. **Navigating the Editor**: When you open the Wix Editor, you'll be taken to a blank version of your template. On the left side of the screen, you'll see a toolbar with various options for adding elements to your site. These options include text, images, buttons, shapes, and more. You can click on any element, drag it to your preferred location on the page, and release it.

2. **Editing Text**: To edit text, click on any text box, and a text editor will appear. You can change the font, size, color, and alignment of your text. You can also add links, bold or italicize text, and adjust the spacing. This feature allows you to create engaging content that aligns with your website's overall style.

3. **Adding Images and Videos**: To add an image or video, click on the "Add" button in the toolbar, select "Image" or "Video," and then choose the source of your media (either from

your computer, Wix's free image library, or a stock photo provider). Once the image or video is placed on the page, you can resize it, reposition it, and adjust its settings, such as opacity or border style.

4. **Customizing Layouts and Sections**: You can change the layout of your pages by adding or removing sections. Wix offers several pre-designed sections, such as about, contact, and services, which can be inserted into your page. You can also adjust the size and structure of these sections by dragging the section borders.

5. **Previewing Your Website**: Before making changes to your site, it's important to preview your work to see how it will appear to visitors. The Wix Editor has a built-in preview function that allows you to see what your site will look like on both desktop and mobile devices. This helps ensure your design looks great on all screens.

6. **Saving Your Work**: Don't forget to save your work frequently! Wix automatically saves your progress, but it's a good practice to manually

save your website as well, especially after making significant changes. This way, you won't lose any progress if something goes wrong.

With these tools, you can create a fully customized website that reflects your unique style and needs. Wix's drag-and-drop editor makes it easy to experiment and see your changes in real-time, so you can make adjustments as needed until your site looks perfect.

By now, you've created your Wix account, explored the dashboard, chosen a template, and learned how to use the Wix Editor to build your website. The next step is to dive deeper into customizing your site, adding content, and refining your design. With these basics under your belt, you're well on your way to creating a website that's uniquely yours!

Chapter 3: Customizing Your Website Design

Creating a website with Wix is an exciting and rewarding process. However, it's not just about getting your site up and running—it's about making it reflect your unique style, personality, or brand. The good news is that Wix provides plenty of tools to help you customize your website's design. Whether you want to tweak the color scheme, adjust the layout, or add new elements, you have complete control over how your website looks and feels.

In this chapter, we'll take a detailed look at the various ways you can customize your website design. We'll cover everything from changing colors and fonts to adding pages, images, and more. Plus, we'll explain how to ensure your website is optimized for mobile devices, so it looks great on any screen size. By the end of this chapter, you'll have a fully personalized website that reflects your vision and works seamlessly across all devices.

Basic Customization Tips: How to change colors, fonts, and images to match your style

The beauty of Wix is that it lets you customize your website design in ways that suit your needs and style. You don't need to be a professional designer to make your website stand out—Wix's intuitive tools make it easy to personalize your site. Here are some basic customization tips to get you started:

1. **Changing Colors**:

   Colors play an important role in any website's design. They help convey emotions, highlight important elements, and create an overall aesthetic that reflects your brand or personality. Wix makes it easy to change the colors of various elements on your site.

   o **Theme Colors**: To start, you can change the overall theme colors of your website. In the Wix Editor, go to the "Design" menu and select "Colors." You'll see a variety of color palettes to choose from, or you can customize your own. This will apply your chosen colors across the entire site, including the background, text, buttons, and links.

- ○ **Changing Specific Colors**: To adjust specific elements, like a button or text box, simply click on the element and use the color options in the toolbar. For example, to change the color of your headings, highlight the text and choose a new color from the editor. This allows you to customize every detail of your site to fit your vision.

2. **Choosing Fonts**:

Your choice of fonts is another way to personalize your website and give it a distinct feel. Wix provides a wide range of font options, and you can change the font style, size, and weight to suit your needs.

- ○ **Selecting a Font**: To change the font of text elements, click on the text box you want to edit. A text toolbar will appear, where you can select a new font from the available options. Wix offers fonts that range from modern and sleek to elegant and traditional, so you can easily match the font to the tone of your website.

- Consistency is Key: It's important to maintain consistency across your website. Try to limit yourself to two or three fonts—one for headings and one for body text. Too many different fonts can make your site look cluttered and unprofessional.

3. Changing Images:

Images are among a website's most important visual elements. They help engage visitors, break up large blocks of text, and provide a visual representation of your content. Wix makes it easy to upload and customize images for your website.

- Uploading Images: To add an image, click on the "Add" button in the editor, select "Image," and then choose the source. You can upload an image from your computer, use free images from Wix's image library, or connect to an external image service. Once the image is added, you can resize it, reposition it, or crop it to fit your design.

o **Image Settings**: Wix also allows you to edit your images directly within the platform. Click on an image to open the settings menu, where you can adjust brightness, contrast, opacity, and more. You can also add image filters to enhance your photos and give your site a polished look.

By making these basic customizations, you can quickly transform your website to reflect your personal style or business identity better.

Adding and Organizing Pages: How to create and structure multiple pages within your website

One of the most important elements of any website is its structure. A well-organized site helps visitors easily navigate through your content and find the information they're looking for. Wix allows you to create and organize pages with ease, giving you the flexibility to build a site that suits your needs.

1. **Creating New Pages**:

   To create a new page on your website, go to the "Pages" menu on the left side of the Wix Editor. Click on "Add Page" to create a new page from scratch. You'll be prompted to choose a page type, such as a blank page, a contact page, an about page, or a portfolio page. Wix also provides pre-designed page layouts that you can use as a starting point.

   o **Naming Your Pages**: Once you've added a page, you'll need to give it a name. Make sure the name is clear and descriptive so visitors can easily identify the page's content. For example, if you're creating a page for your services, name it something like "Services" or "What We Do."

2. **Organizing Pages**:

   Once you've created several pages, it's time to organize them. The easiest way to structure your pages is by creating a navigation menu that links to all the important sections of your website. Wix automatically adds a navigation menu to your site, but you can customize it to match your needs.

- ○ **Customizing the Navigation Menu**: To customize the navigation menu, click on the "Menus & Pages" button in the editor. You can reorder the pages, add new ones, or hide pages you don't want to display in the menu. You can also create dropdown menus to organize your pages into categories, making it easier for visitors to navigate your site.

- ○ **Linking to Pages**: To create links between pages, highlight the text or image you want to link, click on the "Link" button in the toolbar, and select the page you want to link to. This allows you to connect pages within your website and guide visitors through your content.

3. **Adding Anchors**:

For longer pages, you can add anchors to break the content into sections. Anchors allow visitors to jump directly to specific parts of a page, which is particularly useful for landing pages or long blog posts. To add an anchor, click on the "Add" button in the editor, select "Anchor," and position it where you want the section to begin. Then, you can link text or buttons to that anchor, making navigation easier for visitors.

By carefully organizing your pages and structuring them in a way that makes sense to visitors, you'll create a seamless user experience.

Using Wix's Design Tools: A detailed guide on using Wix's built-in design tools to add elements such as text boxes, images, buttons, and more

Now that you've customized your colors, fonts, and pages, it's time to add more elements to your website. Wix provides a range of design tools to help you add text, images, buttons, and other important features. Here's a look at some of the most essential tools in the Wix Editor:

1. **Text Boxes**:

   Text is a crucial part of any website, whether you're writing blog posts, adding product descriptions, or providing information about your services. To add a text box, click on the "Add" button in the editor and select "Text." You can choose from a variety of text types, such as headings, subheadings, and paragraphs.

- **Formatting Text**: Once you've added your text, you can format it using the toolbar at the top of the editor. You can change the font, size, alignment, and color. You can also add bold, italics, or underline to emphasize important words or phrases.

2. **Images and Galleries**:

Images help make your website visually appealing and break up text-heavy sections. To add an image, click the "Add" button and choose "Image." You can upload an image from your computer, select a free image from Wix's library, or use a stock image provider. Wix also allows you to create image galleries, which are perfect for showcasing multiple images in an organized manner.

- o **Image Settings**: Once you've added an image or gallery, you can adjust its size, alignment, and spacing. Wix's editor also offers tools for cropping and filtering images, so you can enhance the look of your photos directly within the platform.

3. **Buttons and Links**:

Buttons are essential for guiding users to important actions, such as signing up for a newsletter, purchasing a product, or contacting you. To add a button, click on the "Add" button, then select "Button." You can customize the text on the button and link it to another page, a URL, or an external website.

- o **Button Style**: Wix offers a variety of button styles, including rectangular, circular, and text-based buttons. You can customize the button's color, font, and size to match your website's design.

4. **Forms and Contact Elements**:

Wix also offers built-in contact forms and other elements that help you interact with your visitors. To add a contact form, click on the

"Add" button, select "Contact," and choose from a variety of form styles. You can customize the form fields, including name, email, message, and more. Forms are great for gathering feedback, inquiries, or customer information.

5. **Social Media Buttons**:

Adding social media buttons is an important way to connect your website with your social media profiles. To add social media buttons, click the "Add" button, select "Social," and choose the platform you want to add, such as Facebook, Instagram, or Twitter. You can then link the buttons to your social media profiles.

Mobile Optimization: Ensuring your website is mobile-friendly and looks great on all devices

With more people browsing the web on their smartphones and tablets, your website must look great on all screen sizes. Fortunately, Wix automatically optimizes your site for mobile devices, but you can make additional adjustments to ensure your site is fully responsive.

1. **Previewing Mobile Design**:

   To see how your website looks on mobile, click on the mobile icon in the Wix Editor. This will open the mobile version of your site, where you can make changes specifically for mobile devices. You can adjust the layout, reposition elements, and even hide certain elements for mobile users.

2. **Mobile-Responsive Settings**:

   Wix automatically adjusts your website's layout to different screen sizes. However, you can further tweak the mobile version by adjusting font sizes, image sizes, and spacing. Wix's mobile editor allows you to optimize your content for a seamless mobile experience, making sure everything from navigation to text readability works well on small screens.

3. **Mobile-Friendly Features**:

   Wix offers several features to enhance the mobile experience, such as touch-friendly buttons, swipeable galleries, and fast-loading elements. These features make it easier for users to navigate your site on their phones or tablets, ensuring a smooth browsing experience.

With these tools and tips, you can fully customize your website to reflect your unique style, add functionality, and ensure it looks great on any device. By paying attention to design details, page structure, and mobile optimization, you'll create a website that not only looks amazing but also provides an excellent user experience.

Chapter 4: Working with Content

The heart of any website is the content it features. Whether you're building a personal blog, a business site, or an online portfolio, content is what connects you to your audience. Wix makes it simple to add and organize content on your website. In this chapter, we'll explore how to add and format text, upload images, and embed videos, as well as how to organize your content effectively. We'll also discuss creating a blog section and adding social media buttons to increase your website's reach.

By the end of this chapter, you'll be comfortable adding the essential elements to your website and organizing your content to enhance user experience and engagement.

Adding Text, Images, and Media: Step-by-step instructions on adding and formatting text, uploading images, and embedding videos

Creating compelling content for your website requires the ability to add various types of media, including text, images, and videos. Wix provides easy-to-use tools that allow you to include these elements, making your website engaging and informative.

Adding and Formatting Text

Text is essential for conveying your message to your website visitors. Whether you're writing an introduction, product description, or blog post, Wix makes adding and formatting text straightforward. Here's a step-by-step guide:

1. **Adding Text Boxes**:

   To add text to your page, click on the "Add" button on the left-hand toolbar in the Wix Editor. Select the "Text" option from the menu, and then choose the type of text you want to add. You'll find options for headings (H1, H2, etc.), paragraphs, and more. Choose the type that fits your content.

2. **Positioning Your Text**:

   Once you've added your text box, you can drag it to the desired location on your page. Wix allows you to move text boxes around with ease, so you can place them wherever they best fit within your layout.

3. **Formatting Your Text**:

To format the text, click on the text box, and a toolbar will appear at the top of the editor. You can change the font, size, color, and style. Wix offers a wide variety of fonts, so you can choose the one that fits your website's style. You can also use options like bold, italics, underline, and alignment to make your text stand out. For added flexibility, you can adjust the line spacing and letter spacing to fine-tune your text layout.

4. **Adding Links to Text**:

Wix also allows you to add links to your text. To create a hyperlink, highlight the text you want to link, and click the link icon in the toolbar. You can then choose to link to another page on your website, an external URL, or even an email address.

Uploading Images

Images play a significant role in making your website visually appealing and engaging. Wix makes it easy to upload and add images to your site:

1. **Adding Images**:

   To add an image, click on the "Add" button on the left toolbar, then select "Image." You'll have several options for uploading images:

   o **Upload from Your Computer**: If you have your image files, click "Upload Images" and select the image from your computer.

   o **Use Wix's Image Library**: Wix offers a free image library with thousands of high-quality images you can use on your site. To access the library, select the "Free Wix Images" option.

   o **Use Stock Image Providers**: Wix also integrates with third-party stock image providers, like Unsplash, so you can find professional-grade photos to enhance your site.

2. **Positioning and Resizing Images**: After adding an image, you can resize and reposition it by clicking and dragging the image's corners. Wix's editor allows you to align your images to the left, center, or right of the page, and you can also adjust the image's padding (the space around the image) for a cleaner design.

3. **Image Settings**:

Wix offers several customization options for images. After adding an image, click on it, and a toolbar will appear that allows you to:

- o **Apply Filters**: You can adjust the brightness, contrast, and saturation of the image.

- o **Crop the Image**: If you want to focus on a specific part of the image, click the crop tool and adjust the frame.

- o **Add Effects**: You can also add effects such as a hover animation, which makes the image change when users hover over it.

Embedding Videos

Videos are an excellent way to engage visitors and provide valuable content. Wix makes it easy to embed videos from YouTube, Vimeo, and other platforms:

1. **Adding a Video**:

   To add a video to your site, click on the "Add" button, select "Video," and choose from the options:

   - **Embed a Video from YouTube or Vimeo**: To embed a video from an external source like YouTube or Vimeo, click on "YouTube" or "Vimeo" in the video menu. Then, paste the URL of the video you want to embed. Wix will automatically pull in the video and place it on your page.

   - **Upload Your Video**: If you have a video on your computer, click "Upload Video" to add it directly to your site.

2. **Customizing Video Settings**:

   Once you've added the video, you can resize it, change its alignment, and adjust the playback settings. Wix allows you to control whether the video plays automatically or only when clicked.

By adding these multimedia elements—text, images, and videos—you can create an engaging and informative website that captures the attention of your audience.

Creating a Blog: How to create a blog section to share updates, tips, or stories

A blog is an excellent way to keep your visitors engaged, share updates, and provide valuable content on your website. Wix makes it easy to create and manage a blog, whether you're writing personal stories, sharing industry insights, or offering helpful tips.

Setting Up a Blog Page

1. **Adding a Blog**:

   To create a blog, click on the "Add" button on the left-hand toolbar, then select "Blog." Wix will automatically add a blog page to your website. If you don't have a blog section yet, you can choose from several pre-designed blog layouts that fit your website's style.

2. **Choosing Your Blog Layout**:

Wix offers several customizable blog layouts, including grid, list, and single post views. Once you've selected the layout that best suits your website, you can adjust the design by selecting different options for font styles, image sizes, and post formats.

Creating Blog Posts

1. **Writing Your First Blog Post**:

After adding the blog, click on "Manage Posts" to start writing your first post. You'll be directed to a text editor where you can add your title, content, and images. Wix's blog editor functions similarly to the text editor we discussed earlier, allowing you to format your text, add links, and upload images.

2. **Adding Categories and Tags**:

To organize your blog posts, you can create categories and tags. Categories allow you to group similar posts (for example, "Travel Tips" or "Recipes"), while tags help users find related content more easily. Be sure to assign relevant categories and tags to each post for better navigation.

3. **Scheduling and Publishing Posts**:

Once your post is ready, you can choose to publish it immediately or schedule it for later. Wix gives you the option to set a specific date and time for when your post should go live, which is helpful if you're planning your blog posts.

Customizing Your Blog

1. **Designing the Blog Page**:

You can customize the appearance of your blog by selecting a theme that matches your site's style. Wix allows you to change the color scheme, font, layout, and even the post display style. You can also adjust the spacing between posts and customize the sidebar to feature categories, popular posts, or a search bar.

2. **Adding a Comment Section**:

If you want to allow your visitors to interact with your blog, you can add a comment section to each post. To enable comments, go to the

"Settings" menu in your blog editor and toggle the option for allowing comments. You can choose to moderate comments before they appear on your site, which helps maintain a positive and relevant discussion.

A blog is a great way to connect with your audience, build authority in your field, and keep your content fresh. With Wix's user-friendly blog tools, you can easily manage and update your blog as often as you'd like.

Organizing Content: How to create an easy-to-navigate content structure, including menus and submenus

As your website grows and you add more content, it's essential to organize your pages in a way that makes navigation easy for your visitors. A well-organized site structure ensures that users can find the information they're looking for quickly and efficiently. Wix provides several tools for organizing your content and improving your site's navigation.

Creating and Organizing Menus

1. **Setting Up Your Main Navigation Menu**: Your main navigation menu is the key to helping users move through your website. To create or edit your menu, go to the "Menus & Pages" section in the Wix Editor. You can drag and drop pages to reorder them, or you can create dropdown menus for grouping related pages. For example, you might have a "Services" dropdown with links to individual service pages, or a "Blog" dropdown with links to categories like "Travel" or "Recipes."

2. **Creating Submenus**:

   Wix allows you to create submenus under your main navigation. To do this, drag a page or link under another page in the menu. This helps keep your site organized, especially if you have a lot of content. For example, under a "Shop" main menu item, you might have submenus for "Men's Clothing," "Women's Clothing," and "Accessories."

3. **Customizing Menu Design**:

   You can change the look of your menu by adjusting its style, color, and layout. To customize the menu, click on the menu in the editor and select "Design." Here, you can choose from different layout options, including horizontal or vertical menus, and adjust font sizes and hover effects.

Adding Search Functionality

To help users find specific content, Wix allows you to add a search bar to your website. To add a search bar, click on "Add" in the editor, select "Search," and choose the style you prefer. A search bar is a simple but effective way to improve the user experience on your site.

Adding Social Media Buttons: How to link your social media accounts to your website for wider reach

Social media is a powerful tool for expanding your online presence and connecting with your audience. By adding social media buttons to your website, you can encourage visitors to follow your accounts and share your content.

Adding Social Media Buttons

1. **Using Wix's Social Media Tools**: To add social media buttons to your site, click on the "Add" button in the Wix Editor, then select "Social" and choose the social media platform you want to link to. Wix supports a variety of social media platforms, including Facebook, Instagram, Twitter, YouTube, and LinkedIn.

2. **Positioning the Social Media Buttons**: Once you've added the buttons, you can position them wherever you want on the page. The most common places to add social media buttons are in the header or footer, so they're easily accessible from any page. You can also add them to the sidebar or within blog posts for greater visibility.

3. **Customizing Social Media Icons**: Wix allows you to customize the appearance of your social media buttons. You can change the size, shape, and color of the icons to match your website's design. If you prefer, you can also choose from a variety of icon styles, such as circular or square buttons, or simple text links.

By adding social media buttons to your website, you can increase your reach and provide visitors with an easy way to connect with you on various platforms.

By following the steps outlined in this chapter, you'll be able to create a visually appealing, engaging, and easy-to-navigate website. Whether you're adding text, images, videos, or creating a blog, Wix provides you with all the tools necessary to showcase your content effectively. And with the addition of social media buttons and an organized content structure, your site will be well on its way to reaching a wider audience and making a lasting impact online.

Chapter 5: Enhancing Your Website with Wix Apps

As you continue to build and personalize your website, you may start to think about ways to enhance its functionality, make it more interactive, and ensure it offers a seamless user experience. This is where Wix's extensive App Market comes into play. The Wix App Market is a powerful tool that allows you to add a wide range of apps to your website, from contact forms and galleries to booking systems and e-commerce features. These apps make it easy to integrate additional features without needing to write any code or spend hours customizing complex elements.

In this chapter, we'll explore and use the Wix App Market, which apps are recommended for beginners, and how to install and manage these apps effectively to enhance your website.

By the end of this chapter, you'll be equipped with the knowledge to seamlessly integrate powerful apps that elevate the functionality of your Wix website.

Exploring Wix App Market: How to find and install apps that enhance functionality

The Wix App Market is a central hub where you can find apps designed to add various functionalities to your website. From simple tools like contact forms to advanced systems like booking and reservations, the Wix App Market offers a vast array of choices that can transform your site into a fully functioning digital platform. Here's a step-by-step guide on how to explore the Wix App Market and find the right apps for your needs:

Navigating the Wix App Market

1. **Accessing the App Market**: To access the Wix App Market, go to your Wix Editor and click on the "Add" button on the left sidebar. Then, click on the "App Market" option at the bottom of the menu. This will open up the Wix App Market, where you can browse through various categories and search for apps by name.

2. **Browsing by Categories**: The Wix App Market is organized into

categories based on functionality. Categories include:

- o **Business Tools**: Apps for adding contact forms, CRM (Customer Relationship Management) systems, booking systems, and more.

- o **Social & Media**: Apps for integrating social media feeds, galleries, and media sharing tools.

- o **E-commerce**: Apps for adding online store features, such as payment gateways, shopping carts, and product catalogs.

- o **Marketing**: Apps for email marketing, SEO tools, lead generation, and more.

- o **Design**: Apps for adding design elements like animations, pop-ups, and sliders.

By browsing these categories, you can easily find apps that suit your specific needs. Wix also features a search bar at the top of the App Market, which you can use to search for specific apps by name or keyword.

Finding and Installing Apps

Once you've found an app that catches your eye, you can click on it to see more details. Each app's page includes a description of its features, user reviews, and installation instructions. Here's how to install an app:

1. **Click on "Add to Site"**: When you've selected an app, click the "Add to Site" button. Wix will then install the app onto your website. Depending on the app, you may be prompted to log in or create an account (e.g., for social media apps or marketing tools).

2. **Customize App Settings**: After the app is installed, you'll be directed to a page where you can configure its settings. Each app will have its own set of options and customizations. For instance, if you install a contact form app, you can specify which fields to include (e.g., name, email, message) and choose where form submissions should be sent.

3. **Positioning the App on Your Site**: Once the app is installed and configured, you can move it around your site. Wix's drag-and-drop interface allows you to reposition the app

easily to fit your design layout. For example, you can place a booking form on your homepage or add a social media feed to your footer.

Updating and Managing Apps

It's important to keep your apps updated to ensure they function correctly and provide access to new features. To manage your installed apps, click on the "App Market" button again and select "My Apps" from the menu. This will show you a list of all the apps you've installed on your website, and you can update or remove them as needed.

Additionally, Wix will notify you when updates are available for your apps, and you can update them directly from the "My Apps" section.

Recommended Apps for Beginners: Apps to make your site more interactive, engaging, and user-friendly

If you're new to website building or just starting with Wix, several apps can help enhance your website and make it more engaging, user-friendly, and interactive.

Here's a list of recommended apps for beginners, focusing on those that are easy to install and customize:

1. Wix Forms

Wix Forms is an essential app that allows you to add contact forms, surveys, and registration forms to your website. Forms are one of the easiest ways to engage with your visitors and collect valuable information, such as customer feedback, event registrations, and service inquiries.

- **Why it's useful**: Forms are crucial for any website that requires interaction with visitors. Whether you're collecting contact information, getting feedback, or booking appointments, Wix Forms provides a simple, drag-and-drop form builder that lets you customize fields, design, and layout.

- **How to use it**: After installing Wix Forms, you can add fields such as name, email, phone number, and message. You can also add custom fields based on your needs, such as drop-downs or checkboxes. Once you're done, the form can be placed anywhere on your site, and all submissions will be sent to your email or stored within your Wix dashboard.

2. Wix Booking

If you offer services that require appointments, such as a salon, fitness center, or consulting business, Wix Booking is an excellent tool for automating the booking process. Wix Booking allows customers to schedule and pay for appointments directly on your website.

- **Why it's useful**: Wix Booking integrates seamlessly into your site, offering a professional and streamlined way to manage appointments. Your clients can choose their preferred services, pick a time slot, and even pay in advance. It saves you time by automating scheduling and payment.

- **How to use it**: Once installed, you can set up different services and define available timeslots. You can also sync your calendar with Google Calendar to keep track of appointments. Wix Booking also allows customers to reschedule or cancel appointments, and you'll be notified of any changes.

3. Wix Photo Gallery

Wix's Photo Gallery app is perfect for showcasing images, whether you're displaying products, portfolios, or personal photos. This app offers a variety of layouts, including grid, slideshow, and masonry, giving you the flexibility to present your images in the best possible way.

- **Why it's useful**: A photo gallery is an essential feature for many websites, especially portfolios, galleries, and businesses that sell products. Wix Photo Gallery offers customizable settings for image sizes, spacing, and animation effects, so you can create an attractive and interactive visual display.

- **How to use it**: To set up the gallery, upload your images, select the layout you prefer, and arrange the photos. You can also add captions, tags, and links to each image, which is great for e-commerce sites that want to link images to product pages.

4. Wix Social Media Stream

If you want to keep your website fresh and engage with your audience, the Wix Social Media Stream app is a great choice. This app lets you display posts from your social media accounts (like Instagram, Twitter, and Facebook) directly on your website.

- **Why it's useful**: Social media is a powerful tool for engagement, and displaying your social media feeds directly on your site helps visitors stay updated with your latest content and activities. It also encourages people to follow you on social media and interact with your posts.

- **How to use it**: After connecting your social media accounts, you can select which platforms you want to display. The app will automatically pull in posts from your social media profiles and show them on your site. You can choose to display specific feeds or aggregate posts from all your social media channels.

5. Wix Chat

Wix Chat is an excellent app for real-time communication with your website visitors. Whether you want to answer questions, provide support, or engage with potential customers, Wix Chat offers a live chat feature that allows you to respond to inquiries instantly.

- **Why it's useful**: Live chat is a key feature for many websites that want to provide fast and personalized customer support. With Wix Chat, you can communicate directly with visitors, increasing your chances of converting leads into customers.

- **How to use it**: Once installed, Wix Chat adds a chat icon to your website that visitors can click to start a conversation. You'll receive notifications when someone initiates a chat, and you can respond from within the Wix dashboard or via the mobile app. Wix Chat also allows you to automate messages, so you can greet visitors or provide quick responses during off-hours.

How to Install and Manage Apps: A guide to managing and customizing the apps you choose

Installing apps from the Wix App Market is simple, but managing and customizing them to fit your website's needs is where the real power lies. Here's a guide to help you get the most out of your apps and keep them running smoothly:

Installing and Customizing Apps

1. **Finding the App**: To install an app, click on the "Add" button in the Wix Editor, select "App Market," and browse the available apps. Once you find an app that you want to install, click on it to view more details, then click "Add to Site."

2. **Configuring App Settings**: After adding an app to your site, you'll be able to configure its settings to suit your needs. Each app has its own settings page, where you can adjust features like display style, layout, content, and functionality. For example, with the Wix Forms app, you can add or remove form fields, change the color scheme, and customize the submission confirmation messages.

3. **Repositioning Apps**: Once an app is installed and configured, you can position it on your page by clicking and dragging it to the desired location. Wix allows you to move apps around easily with its drag-and-drop editor, ensuring the app integrates smoothly into your site design.

Managing Your Installed Apps

1. **Updating   Apps:**
   To ensure your apps stay up-to-date, check for updates periodically. Wix will notify you when an app update is available, and you can install updates directly from the Wix dashboard.

2. **Removing   Apps:**
   If you no longer need an app, you can remove it by going to the "App Market" section and clicking on "My Apps." From here, you can select the app you want to delete and click the trash icon to remove it from your site.

3. **Accessing   App   Support:**
   If you encounter any issues with an app, most have support options. You can visit the app's support page, read FAQs, or contact the app's customer service team for assistance.

By effectively managing your apps, you can keep your website running smoothly and ensure that it offers the best possible experience for your visitors.

Wix's App Market provides an easy and flexible way to add new features and functionality to your website. Whether you're looking to add booking systems, social media feeds, or interactive elements like chat and forms, the apps available in the Wix App Market allow you to enhance your website with just a few clicks. By exploring the app market, choosing the right apps for your needs, and managing them effectively, you'll be able to create a fully customized and engaging website that stands out.

Chapter 6: Setting Up Essential Website Functions

When you create a website, it's not just about having a visually appealing design. The functionality of your website is equally important. A website needs to perform well, be easy to navigate, and allow visitors to interact with you or take actions like making purchases, subscribing to your newsletter, or contacting you for more information. Wix provides powerful tools that allow you to easily set up essential website functions, whether you're looking to add a contact form, create an online store, enable newsletter signups, or optimize your website for search engines.

In this chapter, we'll walk you through the process of setting up some of the most important functions on your website. You'll learn how to add a contact form to facilitate communication with visitors, create an online store to sell products, set up a newsletter signup form to grow your email list, and implement SEO basics to improve your site's visibility on search engines. By the end of this chapter, you'll have a website that's not only visually appealing but also fully functional, interactive, and optimized for search engines.

Setting Up a Contact Form: How to add a contact form for communication with visitors

A contact form is an essential feature for any website. It allows visitors to reach out to you directly, whether they have questions, feedback, or inquiries about your products or services. Wix makes it simple to add a contact form to your website, and it can be customized to suit your needs.

Why You Need a Contact Form

Having a contact form on your website is a professional way for visitors to communicate with you. It's a more secure and organized way to handle inquiries compared to just listing an email address. With a contact form, you can ensure that all the necessary information is collected in a structured way, which helps you respond more efficiently.

How to Add a Contact Form

Here's how you can add a contact form to your Wix website:

1. **Go to the Wix Editor**: Open your Wix Editor and navigate to the page

where you want the contact form to appear. This could be a dedicated "Contact Us" page or any other page where you want to add the form.

2. **Select the "Add" Button**: On the left sidebar, click on the "Add" button. This will open up a menu of various elements you can add to your page.

3. **Choose "Contact" from the Add Menu**: Scroll down to the "Contact" section and click on it. Wix provides several contact form options, including simple contact forms, more advanced forms with multiple fields, and form templates with specific designs.

4. **Select a Contact Form**: Click on the form that suits your website's style and needs. Wix will automatically add the form to your page. You can easily drag it to the desired location on your page.

5. **Customize the Form Fields**: Once the form is placed, you can customize it by clicking on it and selecting "Form Settings." Here, you can add or remove fields, such as name, email, phone number, and message. You

can also make certain fields required, ensuring visitors provide the necessary information before submitting the form.

6. **Design   the   Form**: Wix allows you to customize the look of your contact form. You can change the form's background color, adjust text size, and modify the layout. You can also add a thank-you message that will appear once the form is submitted, or even redirect users to another page on your site.

7. **Connect the Form to Your Email**: In the form settings, make sure to enter the email address where you want form submissions to be sent. This ensures that when someone fills out the form, the information is sent directly to your inbox so that you can follow up promptly.

Managing Submissions

Once your contact form is live on your site, you'll begin receiving submissions. You can manage these submissions from your Wix dashboard. Wix automatically saves all form submissions, and you can view them under the "Form Submissions" section. You can also export the data to a spreadsheet for further use.

A contact form helps you maintain communication with your visitors and gives them a simple way to reach out with inquiries or comments.

Creating an Online Store: Introduction to setting up an online store, adding products, and configuring payments (if applicable)

If you're looking to sell products or services on your website, Wix makes it incredibly easy to set up an online store. Whether you're selling physical items, digital downloads, or services, Wix offers a comprehensive e-commerce platform that's easy to set up and manage.

Why You Need an Online Store

An online store is an essential component for businesses that want to sell their products or services over the internet. Wix's e-commerce tools allow you to reach a global audience and manage your store all from one platform. Setting up an online store with Wix doesn't require technical knowledge, and you can start selling right away with its intuitive drag-and-drop interface.

How to Create an Online Store

1. **Start by Adding an Online Store**: In the Wix Editor, click on the "Add" button and then select "Store" from the menu. This will open a range of store templates. Wix provides templates specifically designed for online stores, making it easy to create a professional, visually appealing shop.

2. **Choose a Template**: Select a store template that best fits your products or services. Wix offers various templates for different types of businesses, including clothing stores, art galleries, and electronics shops. Once you've chosen a template, click on it to add it to your website.

3. **Add Products**: Once your store is set up, it's time to add products. To do this, click on the "Store" tab in the Wix Editor, then select "Add Product." You'll

be prompted to enter information about each product, including its name, description, price, and image. You can also add multiple product variants (such as sizes or colors), stock levels, and product categories.

4. **Organize Your Products**: Wix allows you to categorize your products for easy browsing. For example, you can create categories like "New Arrivals," "Best Sellers," or "Sale Items." You can also set up a product search bar so that customers can quickly find what they're looking for.

5. **Set Up Payment Methods**: To accept payments online, you'll need to set up a payment gateway. Wix offers several options, including PayPal, credit card processing, and Wix Payments (Wix's payment processor). You can select the payment methods you want to use during the store setup process. Wix ensures that transactions are secure, so your customers can shop with confidence.

6. **Configure Shipping and Tax Settings**: If you're selling physical products, you'll need to

set up shipping options and tax rates. Wix provides customizable shipping settings that allow you to define shipping rates based on location, weight, or price. You can also set up tax rates based on your country's tax laws.

7. **Launch Your Store**: Once you add all the products, configure payment methods, and set up shipping settings, your online store is ready to launch. You can preview the store to make sure everything looks good, and then publish your site for the world to see.

Managing Your Online Store

After your store is live, Wix provides tools to manage your orders, track inventory, and handle customer inquiries. You can view order history, update product information, and manage customer accounts directly from the Wix dashboard.

Creating an online store with Wix opens up many possibilities for selling products or services online. Wix's e-commerce tools are user-friendly and customizable, making it easy to set up and manage your online business.

Setting Up a Newsletter Signup: How to create a simple newsletter signup form for your website visitors

A newsletter is a powerful way to keep your audience informed about updates, promotions, or new content. With Wix, you can easily create a newsletter signup form that allows visitors to subscribe to receive updates directly to their inbox.

Why You Need a Newsletter Signup

Building an email list is an effective way to stay connected with your audience and keep them engaged with your brand. A newsletter allows you to communicate regularly with your subscribers, share valuable content, promote products, and even build loyalty with them.

How to Set Up a Newsletter Signup Form

1. **Adding a Signup Form**: To add a newsletter signup form, go to the "Add" menu in your Wix Editor and click on "Forms." Wix offers a variety of form templates, including one specifically for newsletter signups. Click on

the "Newsletter Signup" form and drag it to your desired location on your website.

2. **Customizing the Form**: Once the form is added, click on it to customize it. You can adjust the text, change the button design, and configure the fields. Most newsletter signup forms only require the visitor's email address, but you can also add additional fields if you need more information (such as name or preferences).

3. **Connect the Form to Your Email Marketing Tool**: Wix integrates with popular email marketing services like Wix Email Marketing, Mailchimp, and Constant Contact. You can connect your signup form to these services to automatically add subscribers to your email list. This makes it easy to manage your email campaigns and send newsletters to your subscribers.

4. **Customize the Thank-You Message**: Once someone signs up for your newsletter, you can customize the thank-you message they see. You can also redirect them to a specific page on

your site, such as a thank-you page, or offer a special promotion or discount.

5. **Tracking and Managing Subscribers**: After setting up the form, you can track your subscribers and manage your email list directly from your Wix dashboard. You can view subscriber data, send bulk emails, and monitor the success of your email campaigns.

Encouraging Signups

To maximize its effectiveness, promote your newsletter signup form. Offer incentives for signing up, such as exclusive content, discounts, or free resources. Make sure the signup form is prominently displayed on your site, especially on your homepage or blog posts, so visitors are encouraged to subscribe.

SEO Basics: An overview of Search Engine Optimization (SEO) and how to improve your site's visibility

Search Engine Optimization (SEO) is a crucial part of building a website. SEO refers to practices that improve your website's visibility on search engines like

Google. By optimizing your site, you increase the chances of appearing in search engine results when users search for keywords related to your content, products, or services. Wix provides built-in SEO tools to help you optimize your website and improve its search engine ranking.

Why SEO Matters

SEO is essential for driving organic traffic to your website. The higher your site ranks in search engine results, the more likely users are to click on your site. Proper SEO can lead to more website visits, higher conversions, and ultimately, business success. Wix's SEO tools help ensure that your site is optimized for search engines without requiring technical expertise.

How to Improve Your Site's SEO

1. **Use Wix SEO Wiz**: Wix offers a helpful tool called Wix SEO Wiz, which provides a step-by-step guide to optimize your site. It analyzes your website and provides personalized recommendations for improving your SEO.

2. **Optimize Page Titles and Meta Descriptions**:

Each page on your website should have a unique title and meta description. The title appears in search engine results, while the meta description gives a brief overview of the page's content. Wix allows you to edit these elements easily in the page settings.

3. **Include Keywords in Content**: Use relevant keywords in your website's content, titles, and headings. Keywords are the words or phrases users are likely to search for when looking for information related to your site. For example, if you run a bakery, you might want to use keywords like "fresh bread," "cakes," and "custom pastries" throughout your site.

4. **Optimize Your Images**: Search engines can't read images, so it's important to use descriptive file names and alt text for each image. This helps search engines understand what the image is about and can improve your site's ranking.

5. **Ensure Mobile-Friendliness**: Since many users browse the internet on mobile devices, Google prioritizes mobile-friendly

websites in its search results. Wix automatically optimizes your site for mobile, but you should still test its mobile performance and make any necessary adjustments.

6. **Use Internal Linking**: Linking to other pages on your website helps search engines crawl your site more effectively and provides a better user experience. For example, if you're writing a blog post, link to other relevant posts or product pages.

Implementing these SEO best practices will increase your website's visibility and improve your chances of ranking higher in search engine results.

In this chapter, you've learned how to set up essential website functions, including contact forms, online stores, newsletter signups, and SEO. These tools will help you create a fully functional website that not only looks great but also provides real value to your visitors. Whether you're aiming to sell products, build an email list, or communicate effectively with your audience, Wix's user-friendly tools make it simple to achieve your goals.

Chapter 7: Managing Your Website's Settings

Once your website is up and running, the next crucial step is to manage its settings to ensure it functions smoothly, performs well, and remains secure. Managing your website's settings goes beyond just aesthetics and design. It's about ensuring that your site is properly configured, optimized for performance, and compliant with security and privacy regulations. Wix offers powerful tools and options that allow you to easily manage your website's settings, even if you don't have any technical experience.

In this chapter, we'll cover the key aspects of managing your website's settings, including how to connect a custom domain, track website analytics, secure your site with SSL certificates, and ensure privacy and legal compliance. These settings are essential for creating a professional and functional website that not only meets your needs but also enhances your site's credibility and user experience.

By the end of this chapter, you'll have a fully managed and optimized website that is secure, legally compliant, and capable of effectively tracking its performance.

Customizing Your Domain: How to connect your custom domain name to your Wix website

A custom domain name is the online address where visitors can find your website. It's essential for creating a professional and credible web presence. Having a custom domain (e.g., www.yourbusinessname.com) is much more memorable and trustworthy compared to a free domain provided by Wix (e.g., www.yourbusinessname.wixsite.com). In this section, we'll go through the steps of connecting your custom domain to your Wix website.

Why You Need a Custom Domain

A custom domain is a crucial element for building your brand's online identity. It makes your website look more professional, helps with brand recognition, and makes it easier for visitors to find and remember your site. Additionally, a custom domain helps improve your SEO, as search engines prefer websites with clean and branded URLs.

How to Connect Your Custom Domain to Wix

Here's how to connect a custom domain to your Wix website:

1. **Purchase a Domain Name**: If you don't already have a custom domain, you can purchase one directly through Wix or from a third-party domain registrar such as GoDaddy, Namecheap, or Google Domains. When purchasing a domain, try to choose something short, memorable, and relevant to your brand or business. Wix often offers domain deals for new users, so you may receive a discount or even a free domain for the first year when you sign up for a premium plan.

2. **Access Your Wix Account**: Log in to your Wix account and navigate to the "Domains" section. This can be found under the "Settings" tab in the Wix dashboard. If you purchased a domain through Wix, it will appear in your list of domains here.

3. **Connecting Your Domain**:
If you purchased your domain through Wix, connecting it is simple:

- Go to the "Domains" section and select "Connect a Domain."

- Enter your custom domain name and follow the instructions to complete the setup. If you're using a Wix premium plan, Wix will automatically link your domain to your website.

If you purchased your domain from a third-party provider, you'll need to connect it to your Wix website manually by updating your domain's DNS settings:

- Go to the "Domains" section in your Wix account, click "Connect a Domain You Already Own," and follow the instructions to point your domain to Wix's servers.

- You will need to log in to your domain registrar's account and update the nameserver settings to Wix's default nameservers. Wix provides step-by-step instructions to guide you through this process.

4. **Check Your Domain Connection**: Once you've connected your domain, it may take a few hours for the changes to take effect. Wix will notify you when the domain is successfully connected to your website. You can then type your custom domain into the address bar of any browser to check that your website is live and correctly linked.

Connecting a custom domain to your Wix website enhances your brand's credibility and makes it easier for visitors to find your site.

Setting Up Website Analytics: Understanding the tools available to track visitors and measure your site's performance.

Website analytics are critical for understanding how visitors interact with your site and tracking its performance over time. Analytics provide valuable insights into visitor behavior, traffic sources, and conversion rates, which can help you make informed decisions about improving your site and growing your online presence. Wix offers a range of analytics tools, including its native Wix Analytics and integrations with third-party services like Google Analytics.

Why Website Analytics Are Important

Website analytics allow you to track key metrics such as how many people are visiting your site, which pages they're viewing, and how long they're staying on each page. This data helps you understand what's working on your website, what needs improvement, and where your traffic is coming from. With this information, you can optimize your site's content and layout to improve user engagement and achieve your goals.

How to Set Up Wix Analytics

1. **Access Wix Analytics**: Wix provides a built-in analytics tool that you can access directly from your Wix dashboard. To access Wix Analytics, go to your website's dashboard and click on "Analytics & Reports." This will open a summary of your website's performance, including key metrics such as the

number of visitors, page views, and conversion rates.

2. **View Key Metrics**: Wix Analytics displays your site's traffic data in an easy-to-understand dashboard. You can view detailed reports on:

   o **Website Traffic**: Track the number of visitors to your site over a specific period.

   o **Traffic Sources**: See where your visitors are coming from, such as search engines, social media, or direct visits.

   o **Page Views**: Monitor which pages on your site are being viewed the most, which can help you identify popular content.

   o **Bounce Rate**: This metric tells you how many visitors leave your site after viewing only one page. A high bounce rate may indicate that your site needs improvements in engagement or content.

3. **Using Google Analytics with Wix**: For more advanced analytics, Wix allows you to

integrate Google Analytics, a free service that provides in-depth insights into your website's performance. Here's how to set it up:

- o Sign up for a free Google Analytics account at analytics.google.com.

- o After signing up, Google will provide you with a tracking code. Copy the code.

- o In your Wix dashboard, go to "Settings" > "Tracking & Analytics" and click "+ New Tool."

- o Select "Google Analytics" and paste the tracking code in the provided field.

- o Save your settings, and Google Analytics will begin tracking your site's traffic.

4. **Monitor Site Performance**: Once you've set up Google Analytics or Wix Analytics, regularly check the reports to assess how your site is performing. Look for trends in your traffic data, such as which pages are driving the most engagement and which traffic sources are most effective in bringing visitors to your site. You can use these insights to optimize

your content, improve your user experience, and adjust your marketing strategies.

By using website analytics, you'll gain valuable insights that will help you improve your site and achieve your online goals.

Website Security: Steps to ensure your site is secure, including SSL certificates and privacy settings

Security is a critical aspect of managing any website. A secure website protects visitors' personal information, helps build trust, and ensures compliance with privacy regulations. Wix provides several security tools to help safeguard your site and its data.

Why Website Security Matters

Website security is important for protecting both your site and your visitors. Without proper security measures, your website could be vulnerable to cyberattacks, data breaches, and hacking attempts. Securing your website not only protects sensitive data but also helps build trust with your visitors. A secure website is also crucial for SEO, as search engines like Google prioritize secure sites in search rankings.

How to Set Up SSL Certificates

One of the most important aspects of website security is ensuring your site is protected by an SSL (Secure Sockets Layer) certificate. SSL encrypts the data exchanged between your website and your visitors, making it more difficult for unauthorized parties to access sensitive information.

1. **SSL Certificate with Wix**: Wix automatically provides SSL certificates for all premium users. When you connect your custom domain to your Wix website, SSL is automatically enabled, ensuring that your site is secure with HTTPS (the "S" stands for secure). Visitors will see a padlock icon next to your website's URL in their browser, signaling that the site is secure.

2. **Ensure SSL is Active**: To check if SSL is active on your site, go to your Wix dashboard and click on "Settings." In the "Security" section, make sure the SSL certificate

is turned on. If SSL is not enabled, Wix will provide instructions.

3. **HTTPS and SEO**: Google and other search engines prioritize secure sites (those with HTTPS) over non-secure sites in their search results. Enabling SSL not only protects your visitors but also helps improve your SEO ranking.

Privacy Settings and Protecting User Data

In addition to SSL, Wix provides several privacy settings that help protect your site's data and ensure compliance with privacy regulations. Wix also offers GDPR compliance tools for users in the European Union, ensuring that you meet the necessary privacy standards.

1. **Privacy Policy**: It's essential to have a privacy policy on your website, especially if you collect any personal information from your visitors. Wix provides a privacy policy generator that can help you create a policy that outlines how you collect, store, and use visitor data. You can easily add this policy to

your site by going to the "Legal" section in your Wix dashboard.

2. **Cookies and Tracking**: Wix provides tools to help you manage cookies and tracking on your website. You can choose whether to show a cookie consent banner to visitors, letting them know that your site uses cookies to track behavior. You can also manage how your site interacts with third-party analytics tools like Google Analytics.

3. **Password Protection for Members-Only Areas**: If your website has a members-only area or you want to restrict access to certain pages, Wix allows you to set up password protection. This ensures that only authorized users can access sensitive content on your site.

Regular Security Checks

To maintain your website's security, it's essential to perform regular security checks. Wix automatically updates its security measures, but it's still important to monitor your site for any unusual activity or potential vulnerabilities. Always update your passwords and change them regularly to avoid unauthorized access.

Privacy and Legal Compliance: Basic steps to make sure your website complies with privacy regulations (like GDPR)

When managing a website, it's crucial to ensure that you comply with privacy regulations like the General Data Protection Regulation (GDPR) in the European Union, or other data protection laws that may apply to your region. Wix provides built-in tools to help you comply with these regulations, so your website remains legally compliant.

Why Privacy and Legal Compliance Matter

Privacy and legal compliance are essential for protecting your website's users and avoiding potential legal issues. Many countries and regions have strict laws regarding the collection and use of personal data. Non-compliance can lead to penalties, fines, and damage to your reputation. It's important to ensure that your website is transparent about how you collect, store, and use visitor information.

How to Comply with GDPR and Other Privacy Laws

1. **Create a Privacy Policy**: As mentioned earlier, a privacy policy is an essential document that informs users about how you collect, process, and protect their personal data. Wix provides a privacy policy generator that you can customize based on your needs.

2. **Add a Cookie Consent Banner**: If your website uses cookies, you'll need to inform your visitors and obtain their consent. Wix allows you to add a cookie consent banner that appears when visitors first land on your site. This banner lets users know that your site uses cookies and gives them the option to accept or decline cookie usage.

3. **Enable GDPR Features**: For websites serving visitors in the European Union, Wix provides specific tools to help you comply with GDPR. These tools include features for obtaining user consent, managing data

access requests, and allowing users to delete their personal data if requested.

4. **Ensure Data Protection**: Wix takes security seriously and implements robust data protection measures. However, it's essential to follow best practices when handling personal data. Make sure that any forms you use are secure and that sensitive data is encrypted.

By following these steps, you can ensure that your website complies with privacy laws and protects the personal data of your visitors.

In this chapter, we've covered essential steps for managing your website's settings, including connecting a custom domain, setting up website analytics, securing your site, and ensuring privacy and legal compliance. These settings not only enhance your website's functionality but also ensure that your website is secure, legally compliant, and optimized for performance. With Wix's powerful tools, you can easily manage your site's settings and focus on growing your online presence with confidence.

Chapter 8: Publishing Your Website

Creating a website is an exciting journey, but the final step—publishing your site—is what brings your hard work to life. After months of planning, designing, and customizing, it's time to let the world see your creation. But before you click that publish button, there are a few important steps you need to take to ensure that your website is ready for launch. These steps include previewing your site, testing its functionality, and promoting it to your audience.

In this chapter, we'll guide you through previewing your website before it goes live, publishing it on Wix, testing its functionality, and sharing it with your network. By the end of this chapter, you'll be ready to showcase your website to the world with confidence.

Previewing Your Website: How to preview your website before it goes live

Before you officially publish your website, it's important to preview it in full to ensure everything looks and functions as you intend. Wix provides an easy-to-use preview feature that allows you to see your website as your visitors will. This step is crucial for ensuring that the design, layout, and content are exactly as you want them before you make your website public.

Why Previewing Your Website is Important

Previewing your website helps you catch any mistakes or inconsistencies before they're visible to your audience. It allows you to check for issues with layout, text, images, and functionality, such as broken links or forms that don't work. This step ensures that your website is polished and professional when it goes live.

How to Preview Your Website

1. **Accessing the Preview Mode**: In the Wix Editor, you'll find the "Preview" button located at the top right corner of your screen. Clicking this button will open a live preview of your website, showing how it will appear to visitors when published. You can use this feature to review the entire site or specific pages.

2. **Navigating Through the Preview**: Once in preview mode, you can navigate

through your site just like a regular visitor would. You can click through the pages, scroll through the content, and interact with elements such as forms, buttons, and menus. This gives you a real-time feel of how the website will perform once it's live.

3. **Checking on Different Devices**: Wix allows you to preview your site on both desktop and mobile views. Since many users will be browsing your site on mobile devices, it's important to ensure that your website looks great on all screen sizes. To switch between desktop and mobile views, use the icons at the top of the preview window.

4. **Make Adjustments as Needed**: During the preview, note any areas that need improvement. Perhaps a button is misaligned, an image looks blurry, or the text doesn't display correctly. Make the necessary adjustments in the Wix Editor and preview your site again to ensure everything is perfect.

Final Review Before Publishing

Before moving on to publishing your website, it's a good idea to review the following elements:

- **Design and Layout**: Ensure that the design elements, including colors, fonts, and images, align with your vision and brand.

- **Functionality**: Test interactive elements like forms, buttons, and links to ensure they work as expected.

- **Mobile Responsiveness**: Double-check that your website is mobile-friendly and that content is easily readable and accessible on small screens.

- **Spelling and Grammar**: Carefully proofread your text for any spelling or grammar mistakes. Even small errors can impact your site's professionalism.

- **SEO Settings**: Review your SEO settings to make sure that page titles, meta descriptions, and keywords are properly configured.

Once you're satisfied with the preview, you're ready to publish your site.

Publishing the Site: Step-by-step guide on how to publish your website on Wix

Now that you've reviewed your website and made the necessary adjustments, it's time to hit the publish button. Publishing your website on Wix is easy, and in just a few clicks, your site will be live on the internet.

Why Publishing Your Website is Important

Publishing your website is the moment when all your work finally comes together. It allows you to share your creation with the world, reach your audience, and start achieving your online goals. When you publish your website, it becomes accessible to anyone with an internet connection, giving you the opportunity to grow your brand, attract customers, or share your content.

How to Publish Your Website

1. **Select Your Domain**: Before publishing your site, make sure you've connected your custom domain. If you haven't done so already, you can purchase and connect a domain through Wix or a third-party provider.

Having a custom domain helps establish your brand identity and makes your website more professional.

2. **Click on the Publish Button**: Once you've made all your final adjustments and are ready to go live, click the "Publish" button at the top right corner of the Wix Editor. Wix will ask you to confirm that you're ready to publish your site.

3. **Choose Your Domain**: If you're using a custom domain, you'll be prompted to select it from a dropdown menu. If you're using a free Wix domain (e.g., www.yourname.wixsite.com), Wix will assign it automatically. Make sure you've completed any necessary domain settings before moving forward.

4. **Confirmation of Publishing**: Once you click "Publish," Wix will notify you that your site has been successfully published. You'll be provided with a link to your website, and you can start sharing it with others.

Post-Publication Steps

Once your site is live, you can continue to make changes and updates. Wix allows you to make changes to your website even after publishing it, and those changes will be reflected instantly. You can also monitor your site's performance using Wix Analytics and make adjustments to improve its effectiveness.

Testing Your Website: How to test your site's functionality, including links, forms, and other interactive elements

Before you fully launch your website and promote it to the world, it's essential to test its functionality to ensure everything works properly. This includes checking all links, forms, buttons, and other interactive elements to ensure visitors can navigate your site without issues.

Why Testing Your Website is Important

Testing your website is crucial to ensuring that users have a smooth experience. Broken links, faulty forms, or unresponsive buttons can frustrate visitors and make them leave your site. Thoroughly testing your website before promoting it ensures that everything works as expected and provides a better user experience.

How to Test Your Website

1. **Check All Links**: Go through every page on your website and test all the links. This includes internal links (links that take users to other pages on your site) and external links (links that take users to external websites). Make sure each link works properly and leads to the correct destination.

2. **Test Forms**: If you have any forms on your website, such as contact or sign-up forms, it's important to test them to ensure they are functioning correctly. Please fill out the forms yourself and submit them to verify that the form data is being sent to the correct email address or database. Check if the thank-you message or confirmation page appears after submission.

3. **Test Buttons and Navigation**: Test all buttons on your website to ensure they lead to the correct pages or trigger the right actions. Ensure that your navigation menu is

easy to use and leads to the right sections of your site. Test both the desktop and mobile versions of your website to ensure smooth functionality on all devices.

4. **Check Mobile Responsiveness**: Since a large percentage of website visitors browse on mobile devices, it's crucial to test how your website looks and functions on smaller screens. Use the Wix mobile editor to preview and test your site's mobile version. Make sure text is readable, images are properly sized, and buttons are easy to click.

5. **Perform Speed Tests**: Website loading speed is a key factor in user experience and SEO. A slow-loading website can drive visitors away. Use tools like Google PageSpeed Insights to test your website's loading speed and see if any areas need improvement. Wix automatically optimizes websites for speed, but it's still a good idea to check your site's performance regularly.

6. **Check for Errors**: Scan through your website for any errors or

inconsistencies. Look for issues such as broken images, missing text, or incorrect formatting. Make sure everything aligns correctly and that the design is consistent across all pages.

Final Adjustments After Testing

Once you've tested your website and identified any issues, make the necessary adjustments in the Wix Editor. After making changes, go through the testing process again to ensure everything is working correctly before promoting your site.

Sharing Your Website: How to promote your newly launched website with your friends, family, and social media followers

Now that your website is live and fully functional, it's time to share it with the world! Promoting your website is key to driving traffic and building an audience. Fortunately, Wix provides several tools to help you share your website with your friends, family, and social media followers.

Why Sharing Your Website is Important

Promoting your website helps attract visitors and potential customers, build brand awareness, and increase engagement with your audience. By sharing your website with your network, you can encourage others to visit, share, and interact with your content.

How to Share Your Website

1. **Share on Social Media**: Wix makes it easy to share your website directly on social media platforms like Facebook, Instagram, Twitter, and LinkedIn. After publishing your site, click on the "Share" button in the Wix dashboard. You'll see options to post your website link on various social media platforms, or you can copy the link and paste it into a post.

2. **Send to Friends and Family**: Share your website link with friends and family via email or messaging apps. Personal recommendations from people you know are one of the best ways to spread the word and get initial visitors to your site.

3. **Create a Blog Post or Newsletter**: If you have a blog or an email list, create a post or a newsletter announcing the launch of your website. Share the benefits of your website and encourage your subscribers to visit. You can also offer an exclusive discount or giveaway to entice people to check out your site.

4. **Submit Your Website to Search Engines**: To ensure your website gets indexed by search engines, you can submit your website's URL to Google, Bing, and other search engines. This helps your site show up in search results, making it easier for people to find you.

5. **Monitor Traffic and Engagement**: Once you've shared your website, monitor its traffic and engagement using Wix Analytics or Google Analytics. Look for patterns in how visitors are interacting with your site, and use that information to refine your promotional strategies.

In this chapter, we've covered the essential steps to publish your Wix website, including previewing, publishing, testing, and sharing. With these steps complete, your website is now live and ready to attract visitors. Remember, the launch of your website is just the beginning. By continuously testing, refining, and promoting your site, you can ensure its long-term success and grow your online presence effectively.

Chapter 9: Maintaining and Updating Your Website

Once your website is live and running, the work doesn't end there. To ensure it continues to provide value to your visitors, it's crucial to maintain and update your website regularly. Routine maintenance is essential for keeping your website fresh, secure, and efficient. Additionally, being able to troubleshoot common issues, perform backups, and optimize your website's performance will help prevent problems from arising and ensure that your site remains reliable over time.

In this chapter, we'll cover everything you need to know about maintaining and updating your Wix website. We'll look at the importance of updating content, images, and other elements, how to back up your website data and restore it when necessary, troubleshooting common issues, and tips for improving website performance. By the end of this chapter, you'll be equipped to keep your website in top shape and provide a seamless experience for your visitors.

Routine Maintenance: How to update content, images, and other elements regularly to keep your website fresh

One of the most important aspects of maintaining your website is ensuring that the content remains fresh and relevant. Regular updates help keep your visitors engaged, improve SEO, and keep your website aligned with your current business goals. Routine maintenance involves updating text, images, products, and other elements of your site. Here's a guide to maintaining your site effectively.

Why Routine Maintenance is Important

Website maintenance is essential for several reasons:

- **Relevance**: Updating content ensures your site stays current and relevant to your audience. For example, if you're running a business, keeping product descriptions, pricing, and offers up to date is crucial.

- **SEO**: Fresh content and regularly updated pages are favored by search engines. Search engines like Google rank websites higher when they see that the content is regularly updated.

- **Engagement**: Regular updates to your blog, products, or services keep your visitors coming back. A stale website can lead to reduced engagement, while fresh content keeps users interested and more likely to share your site.

How to Update Content Regularly

1. **Editing Text Content**: Your website's text content should reflect any changes in your business or offerings. To update text, simply navigate to the page you want to edit in the Wix Editor, click on the text box, and make changes directly. This could involve updating service offerings, adding new blog posts, or refreshing product descriptions.

2. **Updating Images and Media**: Images are a key part of your site's visual appeal. If you've changed your branding or have new products to showcase, updating your images ensures that your site reflects the most accurate and up-to-date version of your business.

   ○ **Replacing Images**: To update an image, click on the image in the Wix Editor and choose "Replace." You can then upload a new image from your computer or choose one from the Wix image library.

○ **Optimizing Images**: Ensure that your images are optimized for web use. Large image files can slow down your website's load time, so it's essential to compress images before uploading them. Wix offers automatic image optimization, but it's always good practice to ensure images are appropriately sized for fast loading times.

3. **Updating Product Listings (for E-commerce Sites)**: If you're running an online store, regularly updating product listings is essential for keeping your customers informed. To update a product, go to the "Store" tab in your Wix dashboard, click on the product you want to edit, and update the product name, description, price, or any other relevant details. Don't forget to upload new images if you have updated photos or product variations.

4. **Creating New Content**: Adding fresh content to your website regularly can help keep your visitors engaged and improve your SEO rankings. Consider adding:

   o **Blog Posts**: If you have a blog on your site, write and publish new posts to keep the content dynamic. Share insights, news, or industry updates to engage your audience.

   o **Customer Reviews and Testimonials**: Updating your testimonials section or adding customer reviews can build trust with potential customers.

   o **Special Offers**: If you're running promotions, sales, or limited-time offers, make sure to add them to your site promptly so visitors can take advantage of them.

5. **Updating Calls to Action (CTAs)**: If your website includes calls to action (CTAs), such as "Sign Up," "Buy Now," or "Learn More," it's important to ensure that they're compelling

and up to date. Test the effectiveness of your CTAs regularly and change them to align with your marketing goals.

Setting Up a Content Update Schedule

A good way to stay on top of content updates is to set up a regular content update schedule. Depending on your business, this could involve weekly, monthly, or quarterly updates. For example, if you run an online store, you might want to update product listings and pricing monthly. For a blog, consider posting once a week to maintain engagement.

Backups and Recovery: How to back up your website data and restore it if necessary

Even with the best planning, unforeseen issues can arise that may cause you to lose important website data. Whether it's a mistake during editing, a failed update, or a server error, backing up your website regularly ensures that you can quickly restore it to its previous state in case of data loss.

Why Backups are Important

Backing up your website data ensures that you don't lose content, images, or other elements that you've worked hard to create. Having a backup in place can save you time and effort if something goes wrong and prevent you from losing important information.

How to Back Up Your Wix Website

Wix automatically saves your website as you work on it, which means you don't need to worry about manual backups every time you make an update. However, Wix also offers the option to create a full backup of your site if needed.

1. **Automatic   Backups**:
   Wix saves versions of your website automatically, so you can revert to a previous version if necessary. To view previous versions of your site, go to the Wix dashboard, click on "Site," then click on "Site History." Here, you can view all the saved versions of your website and restore any of them to make your site look like it did at that point in time.

2. **Manual   Backups**:
   To create a manual backup, go to the "Settings" section of your Wix Editor. From there, you can

export your site as an HTML file. While this is a more technical method, it's a good practice to save an offline copy of your site.

How to Restore Your Website from a Backup

If something goes wrong and you need to restore a previous version of your website, follow these steps:

1. **Access Site History**: Go to your Wix dashboard, click on "Site," and then select "Site History."

2. **Choose the Version to Restore**: Scroll through the previous versions of your site and select the one you want to restore.

3. **Click "Restore"**: After selecting the version, click the "Restore" button to revert your site to that previous version. This will overwrite the current version, so be sure to back up any recent changes before restoring.

With Wix's automatic backup system, restoring your website is simple and straightforward, minimizing downtime and allowing you to recover from any issues quickly.

Troubleshooting Common Issues: Common Wix problems and how to troubleshoot them (e.g., broken links, slow loading time)

While Wix makes website management easy, occasional issues may arise that need troubleshooting. Common problems include broken links, slow loading times, and issues with images or forms. Here's a guide on how to troubleshoot some of the most common issues.

Broken Links

Broken links are links that lead to pages that no longer exist or are incorrectly set up. This can create a poor user experience, and search engines may penalize your website for having broken links.

1. **Identifying Broken Links**: Wix provides an easy way to identify broken links by using its "SEO Tools." Go to the "SEO" section in the Wix dashboard, and under "Site Health," you'll find a report on any broken links.

2. **Fixing Broken Links**:
   If you find broken links, go to the page where the link is located and edit it. If the link points to a page that no longer exists, either remove the link or update it with the correct URL. You can also redirect visitors to a new page using a 301 redirect.

Slow Loading Times

A slow website can frustrate visitors and affect your SEO ranking. Wix automatically optimizes your website for speed, but there are still things you can do to make your site load faster.

1. **Optimize Images**:
   Large image files can slow down your website's load time. Use Wix's image compression tools to ensure your images are optimized for web use. You can also reduce the resolution of images that don't need to be high-quality, such as background images.

2. **Minimize the Use of Heavy Elements**:
   Avoid using too many heavy elements on your site, such as large video files or high-resolution images that could impact loading speed. If you

need to use videos, consider embedding them from platforms like YouTube or Vimeo, rather than hosting them directly on your website.

3. **Check Your Website's Performance**: Use tools like Google PageSpeed Insights to analyze your website's loading speed. The tool will provide suggestions on how to improve speed, such as reducing server response time or using browser caching.

Other Common Issues

- **Forms Not Submitting**: If a contact form or newsletter signup form isn't working, check the form settings to ensure they are correctly configured. Test the form to ensure data is being sent to the right email address or database. Sometimes, an issue may arise if the form's fields are incorrectly set or the email settings are misconfigured.

- **Unresponsive Buttons**: If buttons on your website aren't functioning properly, ensure they are linked to the correct page or action. Check the button settings in the

Wix Editor to make sure they are pointing to the right destination.

Improving Website Performance: Tips for making your website run faster and smoother

A fast, smooth-running website is critical for providing a positive user experience and improving your search engine rankings. Slow-loading websites can result in higher bounce rates and lost visitors. Here are some tips for improving your website's performance:

1. **Use Lightweight Elements**: Minimize the use of large images, videos, and other elements that can slow down your website. If you use videos, embed them from platforms like YouTube or Vimeo rather than hosting them directly on your site.

2. **Optimize Images**: Large image files can take a long time to load. Make sure to compress and resize images before uploading them to Wix. Use tools like TinyPNG or Photoshop to optimize your images and

ensure they load faster without compromising quality.

3. **Enable   Caching**: Caching allows your website to load faster by storing a version of your website in the user's browser. Wix automatically uses caching, but you can also enable additional caching for elements like images and scripts to further speed up your site.

4. **Simplify Your Website Design**: Avoid overloading your website with too many elements, such as excessive animations, large files, or multiple third-party apps. Keep your design clean and focused on the most important content.

5. **Choose a Fast Web Hosting Plan**: If your website receives significant traffic, consider upgrading your hosting plan with Wix to improve server performance. Wix offers various hosting options to suit different needs, so selecting the right plan can help boost your site's performance.

6. **Monitor Performance Regularly**: Use tools like Google Analytics and Wix's built-in analytics to monitor your website's performance regularly. This will help you identify areas that need improvement and ensure your website runs smoothly.

In this chapter, we've covered how to maintain and update your Wix website to keep it fresh, secure, and efficient. Routine maintenance, backing up data, troubleshooting issues, and improving website performance are essential for providing a seamless user experience and ensuring that your website meets your goals. By following the tips and guidelines outlined in this chapter, you'll be able to manage your website effectively, troubleshoot common problems, and optimize your site's performance for continued success.

Chapter 10: Going Beyond the Basics

Now that your Wix website is live, it's time to explore more advanced features that will take your site to the next level. While the basic setup is great for beginners, integrating more complex design elements, creating membership features, using external tools, and expanding your online presence can help you create a truly dynamic and professional site. These features will not only enhance the user experience but also give you more control over the functionality of your site and help you reach a wider audience.

In this chapter, we'll dive into how to incorporate advanced design features, create membership areas or subscription-based sites, integrate Wix with external tools, and expand your online presence by adding pages, blogs, and connecting to external platforms. By the end of this chapter, you'll be able to unlock the full potential of your Wix website and enhance its functionality to suit your growing business or personal brand.

Advanced Design Features: How to create more complex elements like animations, custom code, and more

One of the key advantages of using Wix is its flexibility in design. While the platform provides easy drag-and-drop customization for beginners, it also offers more advanced design features that allow you to create a website with sophisticated elements. Whether you want to add animations to make your site more engaging or integrate custom code to add specific functionality, Wix gives you the tools to go beyond the basics.

Why Advanced Design Features Are Important

Advanced design features are important for creating a unique and dynamic website. Animations and custom code allow you to present your content engagingly, enhance user interaction, and provide a more personalized experience. These features can also help improve your site's functionality by adding interactive elements or integrating with other platforms.

How to Add Animations to Your Website

1. **Adding Basic Animations**: Wix allows you to add simple animations to various elements on your site, such as text, images, and buttons. To add an animation, follow these steps:

   - Select the element you want to animate (e.g., an image or text box).

   - Click on the "Animate" option in the toolbar.

   - Choose an animation style from the list (e.g., fade in, slide up, bounce, etc.).

   - Customize the animation by setting the speed, delay, and direction of the effect.

Animations can add flair to your website, making it visually appealing and interactive. For instance, you can animate images to fade in as the user scrolls, or make buttons bounce when hovered over to attract attention.

2. **Creating Scroll Effects**: In addition to basic animations, Wix also allows you to add scroll effects to make your site more dynamic. Scroll effects are animations that

trigger as the user scrolls down the page. To add a scroll effect:

- ○ Select the element you want to animate.

- ○ In the "Scroll Effects" section, choose from options like parallax, fade, or slide.

- ○ Adjust the settings to control when and how the effect occurs as the user scrolls.

Scroll effects are great for creating a smooth, engaging user experience, especially for long-form content like landing pages or portfolios.

Using Custom Code to Enhance Functionality

While Wix is user-friendly and doesn't require coding, the platform also allows you to integrate custom code for added functionality. If you have coding skills or want to add a unique feature to your site, Wix's Velo platform enables you to write JavaScript and use APIs.

1. **Adding Custom Code:** To add custom code to your Wix website, use Wix Velo, which provides a coding environment that integrates directly with your website. To add code, follow these steps:

- Click on the "Dev Mode" in the Wix Editor and enable Velo.

- This opens the code editor, where you can write custom JavaScript code to interact with your website.

- You can add custom forms, buttons, or interactive elements that go beyond the standard Wix features.

Wix Velo also supports the use of external APIs, which allows you to integrate third-party services and create custom apps. For example, you could integrate a payment gateway or a custom chatbot using APIs and custom code.

2. **Adding Custom HTML and Embedding Code**:

   If you're looking to embed third-party content like videos, forms, or other media, you can use the HTML iframe feature. To add custom HTML or embed code:

   - Click on the "Add" button in the Wix Editor.

o Select "Embed" and choose "Embed a Widget" or "Embed Code."

o Paste your custom HTML or code into the provided box and adjust the size and positioning.

This feature is especially useful for embedding content from external platforms like YouTube, Google Maps, or custom forms created on other platforms.

Using Custom Fonts and Styles

Wix offers an extensive range of fonts to choose from, but you can also upload custom fonts to match your branding. To upload custom fonts:

- Go to the "Site Design" section in the Wix dashboard.

- Click on "Fonts" and then "Upload Fonts."

- Choose the font file from your computer, and Wix will integrate it into your website's design.

Using custom fonts and styling elements helps make your website more consistent with your brand's visual identity and ensures that it stands out.

Creating Membership and Subscription Features: How to add membership areas or create a subscription-based website

If you want to create a website that offers exclusive content, features, or services to members or subscribers, Wix provides an easy way to set up membership and subscription-based features. This is ideal for businesses offering premium content, blogs with exclusive posts, or online services that require a subscription.

Why Membership and Subscription Features Are Important

Membership and subscription features allow you to create a dedicated community on your website. By offering exclusive content or services, you can build a loyal audience and generate recurring revenue. Wix makes it easy to add these features without requiring extensive coding knowledge.

How to Create a Membership Area

1. **Enabling Member Signup**: To create a membership area, start by adding a member signup form to your site. Here's how to do it:

    o Go to the Wix Editor and click on the "Add" button.

    o Select "Members" and then choose "Member Signup" to add a sign-up form to your website.

    o Customize the form to collect the information you need, such as name, email, and password.

2. **Customizing Member Pages**: Once you've enabled membership, Wix automatically creates a "Member's Area" where users can log in, access exclusive content, and manage their profiles. You can customize these pages to display the content you want, such as blog posts, videos, or downloadable resources.

3. **Restricting Access to Specific Content**: You can restrict access to certain pages or sections of your website to members only. To do this, go to the "Pages" section in the Wix Editor,

select the page you want to restrict, and enable the "Members Only" option.

4. **Managing   Members**: Wix provides a dashboard where you can manage your members. You can view a list of all users who have signed up, approve or reject membership requests, and send them messages or updates.

How to Set Up a Subscription-Based Website

1. **Adding   Subscription   Plans**: If you want to offer subscription plans, Wix makes it easy to set up payment gateways and recurring billing options. To create a subscription plan:

   o Go to the "Wix Payments" section in the dashboard and choose a payment provider (e.g., Stripe, PayPal).

   o Set up the pricing structure for your subscription plan, such as monthly or yearly billing.

- Offer different membership levels, such as basic or premium, each with different features or access levels.

2. **Delivering Subscription Content**: Once your subscription plans are in place, you can deliver exclusive content to your paying members. This could include access to premium blog posts, webinars, online courses, or downloadable content.

3. **Managing Subscribers**: The Wix dashboard allows you to manage your subscribers by tracking payments, managing subscriptions, and viewing subscriber activity. You can also use Wix's email marketing tools to send promotional emails or updates to your subscribers.

Integrating Wix with External Tools: How to integrate your Wix site with third-party tools for marketing, email campaigns, or analytics

One of the best ways to expand the functionality of your Wix website is by integrating it with external tools.

Whether you want to run email campaigns, track performance with analytics, or integrate social media platforms, Wix makes it easy to connect with third-party services.

Why Integrating External Tools is Important

Integrating external tools allows you to enhance your website's functionality and streamline operations. It helps automate tasks, improve user engagement, and enable you to track important metrics. For example, integrating email marketing tools helps you stay in touch with your audience, while connecting analytics tools lets you monitor your site's performance.

How to Integrate Wix with External Tools

1. **Email   Marketing**: Wix integrates with popular email marketing platforms like Wix Email Marketing, Mailchimp, and Constant Contact. To set up email marketing:

   o Go to the "Marketing" section of your Wix dashboard and choose an email marketing tool.

- Connect your account to the email marketing platform and customize your email templates.

- Add sign-up forms to your website to collect email addresses and send newsletters, promotional offers, or updates.

2. **Google   Analytics**: To track your website's performance and gather valuable insights, you can integrate Google Analytics with Wix. Here's how:

- Sign up for a free Google Analytics account at analytics.google.com.

- In your Wix dashboard, go to "Tracking & Analytics," click "+ New Tool," and select Google Analytics.

- Paste the tracking code provided by Google Analytics into the designated field.

Once integrated, you can view detailed reports on site traffic, user behavior, and conversions to optimize your website.

3. **Social Media Integration**: To connect your website with social media platforms, you can add social media buttons and feeds to your site. Wix allows you to integrate with platforms like Facebook, Instagram, and Twitter. To add social media buttons:

   o Go to the "Add" menu in the Wix Editor, select "Social," and choose the social media platform you want to integrate.

   o Enter your social media profile links to enable visitors to follow or share your content.

4. **Third-Party Apps**: Wix has an extensive App Market where you can find third-party tools to integrate with your website. From booking systems and live chat apps to SEO tools and customer support platforms, you can find apps that suit your specific needs. Browse the App Market to explore available options and easily add them to your site.

Expanding Your Online Presence: Steps to build on your website, such as creating additional pages, adding a blog, or connecting with external platforms

Once your website is up and running, it's time to start expanding your online presence. A well-rounded website often includes multiple pages, a blog, and integration with external platforms to help grow your audience and increase engagement. Here are a few ways you can expand your site:

Adding Additional Pages

As your website evolves, you may need to add new pages to showcase additional content or services. Wix makes it easy to add pages:

1. Click on the "Pages" menu in the Wix Editor.

2. Select "Add Page" to create a new page.

3. Choose from predefined templates or start with a blank page.

4. Organize your pages using the navigation menu to ensure your site is easy to navigate.

Starting a Blog

Adding a blog is a great way to share updates, stories, or insights with your audience. Wix's built-in blog features make it easy to manage and publish posts. You can create a blog by going to the "Add" menu in the Wix Editor, selecting "Blog," and choosing a layout.

Connecting with External Platforms

To expand your reach, consider connecting your website to external platforms like e-commerce sites, affiliate marketing programs, or booking systems. Wix makes it simple to integrate with external tools, allowing you to provide your visitors with a wide range of options and services.

In this chapter, we've explored how to go beyond the basics of Wix by incorporating advanced design features, creating membership and subscription areas, integrating external tools, and expanding your website's online presence. These tools and strategies will help you create a website that is not only functional but also dynamic, engaging, and optimized for growth. With Wix, the possibilities are endless, and by utilizing these advanced features, you can take your website to the next level.

Chapter 11: Troubleshooting and Getting Help

Running a website comes with its challenges, and no matter how easy the process is with platforms like Wix, there will inevitably be moments when things don't go as planned. Whether it's a technical issue, a design problem, or something you don't know how to fix, having the right support at your fingertips is crucial. Wix offers several resources to help you troubleshoot issues, resolve common problems, and get professional assistance when needed.

In this chapter, we will guide you through the various ways you can troubleshoot problems with your Wix website, access additional support through the Wix Help Center, connect with the Wix community for advice, and reach out to Wix's support team for more in-depth assistance. We'll also cover common errors and how to fix them, so you can ensure your website runs smoothly without any roadblocks.

By the end of this chapter, you'll have a clear understanding of how to solve issues that might arise and where to go for help when you need it. Troubleshooting doesn't have to be difficult; with the right resources, you can easily navigate and fix problems as they come.

Wix Help Center: How to access the Wix Help Center for additional support

The Wix Help Center is one of the most accessible resources for finding answers to your questions and resolving issues that may arise while managing your website. It provides a comprehensive collection of articles, tutorials, and step-by-step guides on almost every aspect of using the Wix platform.

Why the Wix Help Center is Essential

The Wix Help Center is the go-to place for quick answers and solutions to a wide range of problems, from basic questions to more advanced issues. It covers topics like design, functionality, SEO, e-commerce, billing, and more. Whether you're experiencing an error or looking to optimize your website's performance, the Help Center is your first stop.

How to Access the Wix Help Center

1. **Accessing the Help Center from the Wix Dashboard**:

To access the Wix Help Center, log in to your Wix account. From the Wix dashboard, look for the "Help" icon, which is typically located in the bottom-left corner of your screen. Clicking on this will open a menu with various options, including a direct link to the Wix Help Center.

2. **Searching for Articles**: Once you're in the Help Center, you can search for articles by typing your query or issue into the search bar at the top of the page. The Help Center provides relevant articles, FAQs, and step-by-step instructions for resolving common issues. This search tool is invaluable if you're looking for a quick fix or specific guidance.

3. **Browsing Categories**: If you're not sure where to start, you can browse the Help Center's categories. The articles are organized into sections such as:

   - **Getting Started**: For beginners, with tutorials on setting up and designing your website.

   - **Design and Features**: For more advanced design tips and tools.

- Site Management: For managing your site's content, SEO, and performance.

- **Billing and Payments**: For issues related to subscriptions, payments, and billing.

- **Marketing and SEO**: For guidance on improving your website's visibility and user engagement.

4. **Step-by-Step Guides and Tutorials**: Many of the articles in the Help Center are accompanied by step-by-step guides and video tutorials. These resources are particularly helpful if you're a visual learner or need detailed instructions for specific tasks, such as adding a contact form, setting up an online store, or troubleshooting errors.

Common Topics Covered in the Help Center

Some common topics you can find in the Wix Help Center include:

- **Designing Your Website**: Articles on customizing templates, adding images, text, and multimedia elements.

- **SEO and Marketing**: Guides on improving your site's search engine ranking, using Wix's SEO tools, and marketing your website.

- **E-commerce Support**: Articles on setting up online stores, managing inventory, and handling payments.

- **Mobile Optimization**: Instructions on making sure your website looks great on mobile devices.

- **Troubleshooting Errors**: Solutions to common errors that may occur while building or managing your site.

The Wix Help Center is a valuable resource for quickly finding answers to common questions and troubleshooting issues before seeking further assistance.

Wix Community Forum: Connecting with the Wix community for advice and assistance

In addition to the Wix Help Center, Wix also has a thriving Community Forum where users can ask questions, share advice, and learn from one another. The forum is a great place to get insights from other Wix users who may have experienced similar issues or have tips to share.

Why the Wix Community Forum is Valuable

The Wix Community Forum is a space where you can connect with a wide range of users, from beginners to experienced designers and developers. Because the forum is open to all Wix users, you have access to a diverse set of ideas, troubleshooting tips, and creative solutions to common problems.

The community aspect of the forum is particularly valuable when you need feedback on design choices, want to explore new features, or are looking for ideas on how to improve your website. It's also an excellent place to find solutions to problems that may not be covered in the Help Center.

How to Access the Wix Community Forum

1. **Navigating to the Forum**: To access the Wix Community Forum, visit the official Wix website and scroll down to the bottom of the page. There, you'll find a link to the "Wix Forum." Alternatively, you can directly

access the forum by typing "Wix Community Forum" into your browser's search bar.

2. **Registering for the Forum**: To actively participate in discussions, ask questions, or respond to other users, you'll need to create a Wix account or log into your existing one. Once logged in, you can post your own questions, reply to other posts, or explore different categories to find helpful content.

3. **Categories and Topics**: The Wix Community Forum is organized into categories that cover various topics, including:

   o **Website Design**: Discussions on design tips, template choices, and advanced design techniques.

   o **Business and Marketing**: Advice on growing your online business, improving SEO, and increasing sales.

   o **Technical Support**: A place to ask about technical issues related to functionality or performance.

- ○ **Feedback and Ideas**: Share your feedback on Wix features or submit ideas for improvements.

4. **Search for Answers**: Before posting a new question, use the search bar to see if someone else has already asked a similar question. Many users post their solutions to common problems, so browsing through previous posts can often save you time.

Engaging with the Community

The Wix Community Forum is designed to be collaborative and helpful. If you have a question, feel free to post it, and other users or Wix experts may respond with solutions. Likewise, if you come across a problem someone else is facing, offering a solution or advice is a great way to engage with the community and build relationships with other Wix users.

Contacting Wix Support: How to reach out to Wix's support team for technical help or guidance

If you can't find a solution in the Wix Help Center or Community Forum, Wix provides professional customer support that can help with more complex issues. Wix's support team is available through multiple channels, including live chat, email, and phone, depending on your support plan.

Why Contacting Wix Support is Necessary

If you encounter an issue that you can't resolve on your own, or if you need more specialized help, contacting Wix's support team is the best course of action. Wix's support staff is knowledgeable about the platform and can provide guidance on a range of topics, from technical issues to billing inquiries. Additionally, for premium users, Wix offers priority support, which allows for faster response times.

How to Contact Wix Support

1. **Using the Wix Help Center**: To contact Wix support, start by visiting the Help Center. Scroll to the bottom of the page,

and you'll find a "Contact Us" option. From there, you can choose the type of issue you need help with and select from available contact options, including live chat or email.

2. **Live** **Chat**:
Wix offers live chat support for many users, which is the fastest way to get help. Live chat connects you with a Wix representative who can provide real-time assistance. To access live chat, go to the Help Center and select the live chat option under "Contact Us."

3. **Email** **Support**:
If you prefer to communicate via email or if your issue requires a detailed response, you can submit a support ticket. You'll need to provide your Wix account details, a description of the issue, and any relevant screenshots. Wix will typically respond to email support requests within a few business days.

4. **Phone** **Support**:
For premium Wix users, phone support is available. If you're on a premium plan, you can find the phone number for customer support in

the Help Center or through your Wix dashboard. When calling, make sure to have your account details and a clear description of the issue so that the support representative can assist you efficiently.

5. **Premium   Support**: Wix offers premium support for users with a Wix premium plan. Premium support includes priority service, faster response times, and direct access to senior support staff. If you're running a business or need more advanced help, upgrading to a premium plan for priority support may be worth considering.

Common Errors and Fixes: A list of common errors users encounter on Wix and how to resolve them

Even the most experienced users encounter errors from time to time. Fortunately, many common issues on Wix are easy to fix with a little troubleshooting. Below are some common errors you may encounter, along with steps to resolve them:

1. Broken Links

Problem: A link on your website leads to a 404 error page or doesn't work at all.

Solution:

- Go to the Wix Editor and check the page where the link is located. Ensure the link is pointing to the correct page or external URL.

- If the page is missing or deleted, either restore the page or update the link to a valid destination.

- Use the Wix "Site Health" tool to scan for broken links and fix them quickly.

2. Slow Website Loading Time

Problem: Your website takes too long to load, which can frustrate visitors and affect your search engine ranking.

Solution:

- Optimize images by reducing file sizes without losing quality. Wix automatically optimizes images, but it's still good practice to manually compress them before uploading.

- Minimize the use of heavy elements, such as large videos, unnecessary animations, or third-party widgets that slow down loading times.

- Test your website's speed using tools like Google PageSpeed Insights and follow its recommendations for improvement.

3. Form Submission Issues

Problem: Forms on your website are not submitting properly, or you're not receiving form submissions.

Solution:

- Double-check the form settings in the Wix Editor to ensure they are configured correctly, including the email address where submissions should be sent.

- Ensure that the form fields are properly linked and that no required fields are left blank.

- Test the form yourself to see if submissions are properly sent. If the issue persists, try re-embedding the form or creating a new one.

4. Missing or Misaligned Content

Problem: Content, images, or text are missing or misaligned on your website, especially after making updates.

Solution:

- Review the Wix Editor to ensure elements are correctly positioned and aligned. Use the "Snap to Grid" feature for precise positioning.

- Check your website's mobile view to ensure elements are properly optimized for smaller screens. Wix automatically adapts your website for mobile devices, but some customizations may need to be adjusted.

- If content is missing, check to ensure it hasn't been accidentally deleted or moved to another section of your site.

5. Payment Processing Issues

Problem: Customers are unable to complete payments on your online store.

Solution:

- Check your payment gateway settings to ensure they are correctly configured. Make sure you've set up your payment providers (PayPal, Stripe, Wix Payments, etc.) properly.

- If you're using Wix Payments, ensure that your account is active and there are no issues with your payment processor.

- Test the checkout process to ensure no bugs or errors are preventing successful transactions.

In this chapter, we've discussed how to troubleshoot common Wix issues, access the Wix Help Center, connect with the Wix community, and reach out to Wix's support team when needed. Troubleshooting is a critical skill for any website owner, and knowing where to go for help can save you time and frustration. By using the Wix Help Center, participating in the community forum, and contacting Wix support, you can resolve issues quickly and keep your website running smoothly.

Conclusion

Building a website is no small feat, and the journey from brainstorming ideas to publishing your site is filled with learning, experimentation, and personal growth. As you stand at the finish line of this process, it's time to reflect on what you've accomplished and celebrate your success. Whether you started this journey to showcase your passion, promote your business, or share your creative work with the world, the fact that you've created something unique is a remarkable achievement.

In this conclusion, we'll take a moment to recognize your hard work, explore the next steps for further improving your site, and point you toward resources to continue expanding your skills. By the end of this chapter, you'll have a clear understanding of how to keep evolving your website and continue to build on your success.

Celebrating Your Success: Encouraging words to recognize the effort and accomplishment of building your website

Creating a website is like building a home for your ideas, a space where your vision can come to life. Whether you're a small business owner, a blogger, an artist, or someone looking to establish a digital presence, what you've accomplished is something to be proud of. You've learned how to design a website, implement features, integrate external tools, and troubleshoot common issues. Most importantly, you've created a platform that reflects your brand, your message, and your goals.

Remember, the process of building a website is as important as the final product. You've gained valuable skills, whether it's learning how to craft a user-friendly design, optimizing your site for better performance, or diving into advanced features like animations, membership areas, and e-commerce integration. These skills are not just useful for your website but can also be applied to future projects, giving you a strong foundation in website management.

Each update and improvement you make to your website will only make it better. Whether you're optimizing for SEO, improving design elements, or adding more content, your website will continue to evolve, and that's the beauty of the digital world—it's always changing, growing, and adapting.

So, take a moment to congratulate yourself. You've invested time and effort into making something that will have a lasting impact on your personal or business goals. Be proud of the effort you've put into your website, and allow yourself to appreciate the accomplishment. Building a website is not easy, and you've done it!

Next Steps: Suggestions for further improving your website, such as expanding its functionality or refining its design

While you've completed the essential steps in getting your website live, the work doesn't end here. A website is a living, evolving entity, and there are always new ways to improve and enhance it. Here are some next steps to consider for continuing to build on your success and take your website to the next level.

1. Refine Your Website's Design

Even after launching your site, design refinement is an ongoing process. As your content grows or your brand evolves, your website design may need to change to reflect these updates.

- **Focus on User Experience (UX)**: User experience is at the core of website design. Review your website's navigation, layout, and content flow to ensure that it's intuitive and easy to use. This is especially important if you've added many pages or new content, as a cluttered site can confuse visitors. Streamline your design to make it user-friendly and visually appealing.

- **Responsive Design**: Ensure your website is mobile-optimized, especially since more and more users browse the web on mobile devices. Wix provides a mobile editor that allows you to tweak your website's design for smaller screens. This is an important step to ensure your site is accessible to all visitors, no matter what device they're using.

- **Typography and Branding**: Consistent typography, color schemes, and branding elements are essential for making your website look professional and cohesive. Consider revisiting your fonts, colors, and overall aesthetic to make sure they align with your branding and communicate your message clearly.

2. Enhance Website Functionality

Adding more functionality to your website can elevate it from good to great. Whether you want to integrate tools that help with customer engagement, improve the user experience, or make it easier to manage content, here are some ways to expand your website's functionality:

- **Adding More Interactivity**: You can make your site more engaging by incorporating interactive elements like quizzes, polls, live chat, or forms. Wix's App Market has a variety of apps that can help you integrate these interactive features without needing coding knowledge. Consider adding a FAQ section, chatbots for customer service, or polls to engage visitors.

- **Membership and Subscription Options**: If you haven't already, you might want to consider adding membership areas or a subscription-based model. This is especially useful if you want to provide exclusive content, access to special features, or offer paid subscriptions for premium services. Membership sites are an excellent way to build a dedicated audience and generate consistent revenue.

- **E-commerce Integration**: If you're running an online store, there's always room to improve your store's functionality. Consider adding more payment gateways, integrating with inventory management systems, or implementing automatic email notifications for abandoned carts. As your product range expands, you may also want to customize the shopping experience to create more personalized recommendations.

3. Boost Your SEO and Content Marketing

Search engine optimization (SEO) is critical for making sure people can find your website online. Improving your SEO can help drive more organic traffic and increase the visibility of your content.

- **Content Updates**: Regularly updating your content with fresh, relevant information is a great way to improve your SEO ranking. This could mean adding blog posts, updating product descriptions, or creating new landing pages optimized for specific keywords.

- **Keyword Research**: Invest time in researching the best keywords for your niche. Use tools like Google Keyword Planner to find relevant terms and phrases that people are searching for. Then, strategically include these keywords in your website's content, metadata, and alt text for images.

- **Link Building**: Backlinks are an important factor for SEO. These are links from other websites that point to your site, and they signal to search engines that your content is valuable. Reach out to other bloggers, influencers, or businesses in your industry and ask if they'd be willing to link to your site or share your content.

- **Analytics Tracking**: Use tools like Google Analytics to track your website's performance. Monitor which pages are getting the most traffic, what keywords are driving visitors, and where your traffic is coming from. This data can help you make informed decisions about where to focus your efforts for further optimization.

4. Focus on Website Speed and Performance

Website performance is crucial not only for user satisfaction but also for SEO. A fast-loading website provides a better user experience and is favored by search engines.

- **Optimize Images and Media**: Ensure that all images, videos, and other media files are optimized for fast loading times. Wix provides automatic image optimization, but you can also manually compress images before uploading them. Use file formats like JPEG for images and MP4 for videos to keep file sizes small without compromising quality.

- **Enable Caching**: Caching can help speed up your website by storing frequently accessed data. This makes it easier and faster for repeat visitors to access your site.

- **Use Faster Hosting Solutions**: Wix's built-in hosting is reliable, but if you experience significant traffic or run a large-scale e-commerce site, consider upgrading to a premium hosting plan. A faster hosting plan can improve your website's load times and overall performance.

5. Expand Your Reach with Social Media and External Platforms

Once your website is optimized and ready, it's time to focus on expanding your online presence. Promoting your site across different platforms and connecting with more people can help you reach a wider audience.

- **Social Media Integration**: Use social media platforms like Facebook, Instagram, Twitter, and LinkedIn to drive traffic to your site. Share updates, blog posts, or promotional offers to keep your followers engaged and encourage them to visit your website. Wix makes it easy to integrate social media buttons on your website, allowing visitors to follow you with just one click.

- **Email Marketing**: Building an email list is another great way to promote your website. Use Wix's email marketing tools or connect to external platforms like Mailchimp or Constant Contact to create newsletters, announcements, or product updates. Personalizing your emails and offering special deals can increase engagement and conversion rates.

- **Collaborations and Guest Posts**: If you're looking to expand your reach even further, consider partnering with other bloggers, influencers, or businesses in your industry. Guest posting on other websites or collaborating with others on social media can help you tap into their audience and attract more visitors to your site.

Resources for Continued Learning: Where to find more resources to continue improving your website-building skills

Website building is an ongoing learning process. Whether you're a beginner or an experienced user, there's always room for growth and improvement. Thankfully, there are plenty of resources available to help you continue developing your skills and knowledge. Here are some great places to continue your learning journey:

1. Wix Learning Resources

- **Wix Academy**: Wix offers a comprehensive online learning platform called Wix Academy, where you can access free courses and tutorials. These courses cover everything from basic website building to advanced techniques like SEO, e-commerce management, and marketing strategies.

- **Wix Blog**: The Wix blog is regularly updated with tips, tutorials, and case studies to help you grow your website. You can learn about trends in web design, new features in Wix, and best practices for improving your site's performance.

2. Online Courses and Tutorials

- **Udemy**: Udemy offers a wide range of courses on web design, SEO, digital marketing, and more. Some of these courses focus specifically on Wix, teaching you how to take full advantage of its features.

- **Coursera**: For more in-depth learning, Coursera provides courses in web development, digital marketing, and design. Many of these courses are taught by experts from universities and companies like Google and IBM.

- **YouTube**: There are countless YouTube channels dedicated to teaching website building and design. Channels like "Wix Tutorial" and "Wix Training Academy" offer video tutorials on everything from basic design to advanced features and integrations.

3. Books and eBooks

For those who prefer reading, there are many books and eBooks that cover topics related to website building, digital marketing, and SEO. Some popular options include:

- **"The Complete Web Developer's Guide"**: A comprehensive book that covers all aspects of web development, including design, coding, and optimization.

- **"SEO 2021: Learn Search Engine Optimization with Smart Internet Marketing Strategies"**: This book offers practical advice on how to improve your website's SEO, which is essential for attracting more visitors.

- **"Don't Make Me Think" by Steve Krug**: A classic book on web usability and user experience, perfect for those looking to refine their website's design and functionality.

4. Forums and Communities

- **Wix Community Forum**: The Wix Community Forum is a great place to interact with other website builders, ask questions, and share experiences. Many experienced Wix users are happy to offer advice and solutions to common problems.

- **Stack Overflow**: For technical questions, Stack Overflow is a widely recognized community of developers who can help you with coding, API integrations, and more.

5. SEO and Marketing Blogs

- **Moz Blog**: Moz is a leading authority on SEO and digital marketing. Their blog provides actionable tips, guides, and the latest trends in search engine optimization.

- **Neil Patel's Blog**: Neil Patel's blog is a valuable resource for learning about SEO, digital marketing, and social media. It provides detailed tutorials and case studies that can help you grow your website's visibility online.

In this last chapter, we've discussed the importance of celebrating your success, the next steps you can take to continue improving your website, and valuable resources for further learning. Building and maintaining a website is a dynamic process, and there's always room for growth. By using the tools and resources available to you, you can continue enhancing your website, expanding your online presence, and achieving your goals. Remember, the web development journey doesn't end with the launch—it's a continual process of learning, improving, and evolving. Keep pushing forward, and your website will only get better over time.

www.ingramcontent.com/pod-product-compliance
Lightning Source LLC
La Vergne TN
LVHW051236050326
832903LV00028B/2431